*e-book*

Creating a culture of ideas is a lot more complicated than letting your corporate Archimedes take a bath. Mercifully, after spending the last decade helping hundreds of companies become more innovative, Dr Amantha Imber has come up with a step-by-step, actionable guide to getting more breakthroughs out of your business. Backed up by interviews with a who's-who of corporate forward-thinkers, I'd urge Amantha's guide upon any executive — we need this book now.

— **Michael Bailey**, Editor, *BRW*

Amantha Imber's *The Innovation Formula* demystifies innovation in a way that any business — from startups to the biggest corporations — will find useful. Imber uncovers strategies that individuals, teams, and leaders of businesses can use to build an innovative culture and mines the gems from real-life innovation experiments at some of the world's most successful businesses. If you need a guide to get innovation going in your business, this is it.

— **Joanne Gray**, Editor, *BOSS* magazine,
*The Australian Financial Review*

A fascinatingly scientific and clear approach to creating that all-important culture of innovation within a workforce.

— **Chris Kreinczes**, Editor and Creative Director,
Springwise.com

Imber has 'democratised' innovation, making it accessible for everyone. *The Innovation Formula* cuts through all the dense, hard to implement research and provides an accessible and actionable primer for creating an innovative culture. If you read just book on innovation, make it this one.

— **Rachael Neumann**, Senior Director of Strategy,
Eventbrite

Reading this book I started to think how I might describe it to others. I originally thought it was like a juicy peach, which oozed irresistible innovation juice. I read more and believed this book to simply be a shining gem reflecting innovation opportunity into the readers' mind. I then finished the book and realised I have just discovered the most powerful innovation and leadership toolkit that will be by my side for the rest of my career.

—**Christopher Stubbs**, Manager, Brand and Innovation,
Virgin Australia

The science of creating an innovative culture delivered in a practical, real-life way you can use immediately.

—**James Thomson**, Companies and Markets Editor,
*The Australian Financial Review*

*The Innovation Formula* is not just another innovation book. It gives practical and relevant examples of what it truly takes to make innovation part of a company's culture.

—**Michael Vavakis**, Group Head of
Human Resources, Lendlease.

*The Innovation Formula* achieves what few books do—it provides an equally valuable guide to both the experienced innovator as well as those new to the field. I wish I had read this book years ago as it would have helped me avoid the mistakes I made along the way.

—**Peter Williams**, Chief Edge Officer, Deloitte

# THE
# *innovation*
# FORMULA

## THE 14 SCIENCE-BASED KEYS FOR CREATING A CULTURE WHERE INNOVATION THRIVES

### DR AMANTHA IMBER

## WILEY

First published in 2016 by John Wiley & Sons Australia, Ltd
42 McDougall St, Milton Qld 4064
Office also in Melbourne

Typeset in 12.5/14.5 pt Bembo Std by Aptara, India

© Inventium Pty Ltd ATF Inventium Trust 2016

The moral rights of the author have been asserted

National Library of Australia Cataloguing-in-Publication data:

| | |
|---|---|
| Creator: | Imber, Amantha, 1977- author. |
| Title: | The Innovation Formula: the 14 science-based keys for creating a culture where innovation thrives / Amantha Imber. |
| ISBN: | 9780730326663 (pbk.) |
| | 9780730326687 (ebook) |
| Notes: | Includes index. |
| Subjects: | Organizational change. |
| | Technological innovations. |
| | Research. |
| Dewey Number: | 658.406 |

Cover design by Wiley

Light bulb cover image by © Chones/Shutterstock; formulas and equations cover image by © BORTEL Pavel — Pavelmidi/Shutterstock

Cover art direction by Lars Wannop

10 9 8 7 6 5 4 3 2 1

**Disclaimer**
The material in this publication is of the nature of general comment only, and does not represent professional advice. It is not intended to provide specific guidance for particular circumstances and it should not be relied on as the basis for any decision to take action or not take action on any matter which it covers. Readers should obtain professional advice where appropriate, before making any such decision. To the maximum extent permitted by law, the author and publisher disclaim all responsibility and liability to any person, arising directly or indirectly from any person taking or not taking action based on the information in this publication.

*For Shannon. And for Frankie,*
*our joint (and best) innovation.*

# CONTENTS

# ABOUT THE AUTHOR

Dr Amantha Imber is an innovation psychologist, a best-selling author, and the founder of Australia's leading innovation consultancy, Inventium. Inventium has been recognised as one of Australia's fastest growing companies in the *BRW* Fast 100 list, and was also awarded the *BRW* Client Choice Award for Best Management Consultancy in Australia.

With a PhD in organisational psychology, Amantha has helped companies such as Google, Coca-Cola, Disney, Lego, Red Bull, American Express, McDonald's, Virgin Australia, Commonwealth Bank and many others innovate more successfully. Amantha was a finalist in the 2015 Telstra Business Women's Awards.

Amantha is the cocreator of the *BRW* Most Innovative Companies list, an annual list compiled by Inventium that ranks Australia's top innovators. She has written for publications including *The Australian Financial Review, BRW, Australian Business Solutions* and *Smart Company* and is the author of the best-selling book *The Creativity Formula: 50 scientifically proven creativity boosters for work and for life.*

Amantha had an international record deal for her debut album *Like Samantha without the S*, prays to the God of Kevin Spacey and claims to have once been freakishly good at table tennis.

Visit inventium.com.au to find out more about Amantha and her team at Inventium, what they do and what they've been thinking about lately. You can also find Amantha on Twitter (@amantha) and via her website at www.amanthaimber.com.

# ACKNOWLEDGEMENTS

I don't know about you, but I am the sort of person who loves reading the Acknowledgements section of books! As such, I spent an inordinate amount of time writing this section because a) books don't get written without a lot of help and support from others and b) because I am a big fan of Acknowledgements sections.

First, you would not be reading this book if it were not for Kristen Hammond at Wiley. Kristen, thank you for believing that people would be interested in what I had to write and for being so liberal with your compliments and encouragement along the journey. Thanks also to the rest of the amazing team at Wiley, including Ingrid Bond, Chris Shorten, Alice Berry, Peter Walmsley and Theo Vassili.

Thank you to Jane Thompson, my amazing editor, who made me sound way more succinct and articulate than I actually am!

A big thank-you to Chad Dickerson, Dae Mellencamp, Stuart Smith, Barry Gold, Christine Gilroy, Megan Kachur, Derek O'Donnell, Hugh Molotsi, Mike Finch, Neil Christie, Kirsten O'Doherty, Evan Cohen, Mariah Monaghan, Tiziana Bianco and Wendy Mayer. I am indebted to you for your generosity with your stories and your time. The examples you gave me about what you are each doing in your organisations was inspiring to me, and I am sure are just as inspiring to the book's readers.

Thanks to Jason Fox, who introduced me to the wonderful team at Wiley in the first place, and for being someone I could moan to about the stress of writing a book and running a busy consultancy at the same time.

Thank you to the hundreds of researchers cited in this book. Without the countless hours and mammoth effort that go into conducting research, this book would have consisted of shoddy advice that may or may not have worked. And thank you to my research assistants, Kash and Themis, for helping me uncover a lot of the great research that went into this book.

A huge thank-you to my team at Inventium. You are my favourite part of what I do and I learn so much from you all every single day. I look forward to Mondays because it means I get to hang out with such an amazing, diverse, quirky, funny and clever gang of people. An extra-special thank-you to Michelle Le Poidevin and to Shelley Logan. Mish, you are the best personal assistant anyone could ever hope for — and damn you for being so good that I had to promote you. Shell, you have taught me so much in the three years we have worked together and I can't wait until you are back from sailing around the world so we can continue the journey.

Thank you to Inventium's clients, who allow my team and I to apply our research and methodologies. You truly are the best group of clients that consultants could ever hope for—you are smart yet humble, and are true innovators yourselves.

A massive thank-you to my mum, Doris, who gave me the writing gene in the first place. Thank you for editing the very first draft of this book and making it infinitely better with all your suggestions. Thank you to my dad, Martin, who also fastidiously looked over the very first draft of this book and put all of his and Mum's changes into a Word document (which was no small feat, considering my mum is computer 'challenged' and there were a lot of red marks over the first draft of this book). Thank you both for being my biggest fans, for bringing me up to have a passion for both science and creativity, and for instilling in me that I could be anything I wanted to be.

Thank you to my amazing husband, Shannon, who walked to get me chai lattes every single Saturday and Sunday morning as I sat at home on my MacBook working on this book while our daughter, Frankie, slept soundly. Thank you for being one of those rare men who truly does treat parenthood and household chores as a partnership, which in turn has given me the time to run Inventium and write a book and be a mum (and also a wife, somewhere in the mix!). What I do would simply not be possible without you.

And finally, thank you to the most amazing little girl a mum could ever hope for. Frankie, you make me laugh and smile so much every single day. And without your amazing superpower of being the world's best and most predictable little sleeper, this book would most definitely not have been written.

# INTRODUCTION

My very first 'adult' job—and by 'adult' job I mean that it was not the one that involved dressing up as a witch waitress at Witches in Britches, or the job sewing hats for a local clothing store, or the job singing and playing guitar for people who had consumed a few too many beers in pubs—was as the human resources manager (HRM) for an Australian security firm. I was in the final stages of completing my doctoral thesis in organisational psychology and was excited to enter the world of full-time office working.

I knew little about the security industry (which was probably a good thing, as I am not sure I would have accepted the job if I had known more), but I knew a lot about human resources and the 'people' side of work from all my studies. I was (naively) ready to transform this security firm into the best place to work in Australia. The last HRM had resigned—I didn't ask why—and my first priority was to recruit as many top-quality security guards as I could, as quickly as possible. There was no shortage of work, but there was a shortage of good staff.

My days were mostly spent in interviews with potential security personnel. I would ask them a series of questions, evaluate their answers, and then make a recommendation to management as to whether we should hire them. Someone from the management team would then conduct a final interview and make a decision.

I was enjoying my job, although it was a little repetitive with such a big focus on recruitment. I felt very grown up going to work in an office every day, wearing a suit (incidentally, this was the only job I have ever had where I had to wear a suit) and feeling as if I were having an impact on a relatively large security firm.

But then everything changed. It all started as a pretty standard job interview. I was interviewing a young man—let's call him Bruce—who had applied for a job as a security guard. Bruce had just completed his certificate in security and this was going to be his very first job as a security guard. I asked him the standard series of questions, and things were going well. His answers were satisfactory and he appeared to be suitable for a role. The interview came to a close, and as I was showing Bruce to the door I noticed he was wearing an earring in his left ear. 'Just to let you know', I said, 'you'll need to take your earring out when you are working—earrings are a bit of a safety hazard'.

Suddenly I found myself shoved against the wall with Bruce gripping my shoulders and shouting in my face, 'No-one tells me what to wear or what not to wear'. He then stormed out of the office. Needless to say, my recommendation was not to hire him.

A couple of weeks later, I was looking across our rosters to see which of my new recruits had been lined up with work already. There were a few familiar names, which was great to see. But then my heart skipped a beat. Bruce's name was on one of the rosters. I immediately stormed into my manager's office.

'Why is Bruce on our roster?' I practically shouted.

My manager, Brendan, looked confused. 'Because we hired him', he said.

'Well, that's obvious—but don't you remember what Bruce did? He assaulted me in the interview.'

'Yes', Brendan said. 'But aside from that, he seemed very good.'

I handed in my resignation the next day.

I moved out of security and into advertising. My first job in advertising was as a consumer psychologist. This involved understanding why consumers behaved in the ways they did and helping brands understand how to use these insights to sell more products. Intellectually rewarding, but not particularly ethically rewarding. I worked in the Melbourne office of a multinational agency and, while the workplace culture was significantly better than at the security firm, my boss unfortunately wasn't.

My first annual performance review is one of my clearest memories of my time at the agency. My manager had suggested we go to a café around the corner, and she was waiting for me at one of the corner tables. I was expecting a glowing review. I had worked my bum off all year and felt that I had done some great work for my clients and my teammates. I had also secured a weekly column in one of the top trade magazines where I wrote about the science of consumer behaviour—great exposure for the agency (or so I thought). So you can imagine my surprise when my boss started off my review by saying, 'You need to cancel your column. The public focus needs to be on me—not on you. And please don't call yourself a consumer psychologist in the media, because that is not your job title'. The review went downhill from there.

I ignored her request, and the column continued for another four years until I made the decision to retire it. Shortly after my review, I was headhunted to Sydney to work for another global advertising agency—Leo Burnett.

They say third time's a charm, and it definitely was for me. Leo Burnett Sydney was on a high during my time there (not because of me—I just had good timing). The agency's creative work was picking up award after award, including several at Cannes (arguably the most prestigious industry awards in the world), and I was lucky enough to work under the leadership of CEO Nigel Marsh.

My boss, Todd Sampson, loved my column. Far from asking me to get rid of it, it was one of the reasons he headhunted me. He asked me to do more writing—not less. I was given the perfect mix of freedom and support by Todd and the teams with which I worked. I felt challenged by my work on a daily basis and was intellectually stimulated by my teammates and my clients. Innovation was actively encouraged by Nigel and his leadership team and great ideas were listened to and supported.

It was during this time that I began to really appreciate the importance of workplace culture to creative output. The culture was so vastly different from the previous two workplaces I had experienced. So when I left advertising several years later to start Inventium, the innovation consultancy I have been running for the past eight years, one of my many missions was to understand the science behind creating cultures where innovation thrives.

★★★

Most weeks at Inventium I speak with groups of business leaders who want to grow their organisations and who recognise that innovation is a sure-fire way to do that. And as we talk, the following question inevitably pops up: 'How do I create a culture for innovation?' I love being asked this question, because it is an area where the latest scientific research tells us very clearly what works and what doesn't. And sadly, the right path is usually the exact opposite of the path most of those organisations are taking.

Many leaders who have been given the directive to 'build a culture of innovation' immediately think about the Googles and Apples of the world. Images of beanbags and table-tennis tables fill their minds, as do 'blue-sky' workshops in far-off country retreats. However, what we know from the research is that all this is completely ineffective in creating a culture of innovation.

As is often the case, the voice of popular culture and fad-ridden management books wins out over the voice of scientific research. Jargon-filled, densely written journal papers are harder to access than the pop-psych books filling the shelves. This book aims to remedy that—to give you a clear, practical understanding of what has been scientifically proven to create a culture of innovation. And it's got nothing to do with beanbags.

*The Innovation Formula* takes you on a journey through the essence of more than a hundred scientific studies into what actually creates a culture of innovation. It looks at the impact of the individual, teams, leaders and the organisation. It tells you how organisations such as Etsy, Coca-Cola, GE and Disney are actively applying these principles to deliberately and successfully create cultures where innovation thrives.

★★★

Research into the field of innovation is flourishing and it's exciting, so let's get into that science right away. There's a concept within academia of the 'hero study'—the study that other researchers in the field cite and refer to. A study becomes the hero study either because it breaks new ground in a research area, or because it brings together many disparate studies and makes sense of a lot of data. The hero study in the area of innovation culture research does the latter.

In the 2007 study 'Climate for creativity: A quantitative review', Samuel Hunter, from the University of Oklahoma, and his colleagues Katrina Bedell and Michael Mumford set out to understand which variables had the biggest impact on innovation culture and conducted an extremely comprehensive literature search.

They started by looking at the general review articles that had been published, then looked through all issues of the major academic journals that focused on innovation and creativity. They then searched all of the main research databases, and then reviewed all conference programs from major psychology and management fields to identify any conference papers that had been presented on the topic but had not yet been published.

But even that wasn't enough. Hunter feared that by looking only at published studies they might miss out on research where the effect sizes had been weak (and therefore not 'worthy' of publication). So Hunter and his teammates used their literature review to identify academics who had published at least two articles on creativity and culture over the previous ten years. They were all contacted and asked for any unpublished papers on the topic.

This comprehensive search uncovered 88 articles, conference papers and manuscripts. A psychologist then reviewed each of these articles and eliminated the ones that did not have sound methodology, did not specifically focus on the relationship between culture and creativity and innovation, and were not quantitative in nature. This whittled the number of papers down to 42, representing data from a total of 14 490 participants.

The data was crunched, and what came out the other end was a set of 14 variables that held up as having a significant impact on innovation culture. All of these variables are discussed in various ways in the chapters of this book.

★★★

In addition to Hunter's meta-analysis, *The Innovation Formula* draws on several other meta-analyses and individual studies that have revealed the most important drivers of innovation culture. These drivers are covered in four separate parts within this book.

Part I looks at what you, the individual, need to be doing. This covers variables that can be influenced at the individual level. If you are a manager reading this book, you can use these chapters to help mentor and coach the people in your team more effectively. You can also use these chapters to reconsider how you structure people's roles, projects and rewards. And if you have no managerial responsibilities, then you can use the chapters in part I to reflect on your own role and projects, and for ideas on how to change what you do to help inject greater creativity into your job.

Part II delves into the team level. There is a variety of innovation drivers that can be manipulated within teams. If you are a manager leading small or large teams of people, these chapters will be useful for thinking about the types of variables that need to be present within your team. You can reflect on the type of culture that currently exists within your team, and use these chapters for ideas on what you can change and improve. If you are not a manager, you can use these chapters to influence at the grassroots level how your team works. Whether you work in a team of two or a team of 20, there are many ideas here that you can integrate into the way your team functions.

Part III examines creating a culture that supports innovation at the leadership level. The research and advice contained here is in the form of tangible recommendations and examples for leaders who are trying to foster a culture of innovation within their organisation, department or team. Even if you don't have official leadership responsibilities, the tips in these chapters will transform you into a leader who inspires people to innovate.

Part IV focuses on variables that need to be present across the entire organisation to affect innovation culture. These are arguably the most challenging to influence, given the reach they need to have. If you are a leader you can use these chapters to help other leaders within your organisation focus on the activities that truly build and foster a culture of innovation. And if you don't have managerial responsibilities, then these chapters will educate you on the seeds you need to be planting to create change.

The final chapter of this book provides advice on what to do next, suggesting concrete steps towards being a change agent for innovation culture within your organisation.

★★★

At this point, you may be wondering about the best way to digest all of the 14 factors that drive innovation culture. And, after reading all those chapters, what is the best way to actually start driving 14 culture changers all at once?

Let me present you with a couple of options:

1   In Hunter's meta-analysis of the strongest drivers of an innovation culture, the researchers crunched the data in a way that ranked the variables from most to least impactful. Obviously, all of them have an impact—and a significant one at that. But if you want to focus on the most impactful variables, focus on chapters 1, 4, 8, 11 and 12.

2   Complete the basic Innovation Culture Audit survey. The audit asks you a series of questions that represent the cultural factors reported in this book. By understanding the current strengths and weaknesses of your organisation you will be able to effectively prioritise your innovation efforts.

So in the spirit of innovation, I encourage you to learn more about the science of creating a culture where innovation thrives, and come out the other end armed to make changes to transform your organisation and the way you work. No matter how big or small those changes may be, you can be sure that they will have a significant effect on improving the innovation output of your organisation.

# INNOVATION CULTURE AUDIT

To get a quick snapshot of how the culture of your organisation performs across the dimensions that matter, take a few minutes to complete this questionnaire.

Please rate your agreement with each item on a scale of 1 to 5, where 1 = strongly disagree, 2 = disagree, 3 = neither agree nor disagree, 4 = agree, and 5 = strongly agree.

### Individual-level factors

| | | |
|---|---|---|
| 1 | People are adequately challenged in their roles — not so little that they are bored and not so much that they are overwhelmed. | |
| 2 | I'm excited by the challenges I face in my role. | |
| 3 | People in my organisation have the freedom to complete their tasks in any way that they see fit. | |
| 4 | I have a sense of control over my work. | |
| 5 | In my organisation, people's efforts in generating and implementing creative ideas are recognised. | |
| 6 | I receive recognition for my innovation efforts. | |
| | **subtotal** | |

## Team-level factors

| | | |
|---|---|---|
| 7 | My team actively shares diverse viewpoints and opinions, even if they are conflicting. | |
| 8 | I feel comfortable expressing an opposing opinion to others in my team. | |
| 9 | My team really listens when we share new ideas. | |
| 10 | In my team, people are very supportive of my ideas. | |
| 11 | In my organisation, collaboration across departments is a common occurrence. | |
| 12 | My organisation often collaborates with other types of companies, such as universities and start-ups. | |
| | **subtotal** | |

## Leader-level factors

| | | |
|---|---|---|
| 13 | My manager encourages me to come up with new ideas. | |
| 14 | My manager encourages me to implement my new ideas. | |
| 15 | Leaders don't just pay lip-service to innovation, they practise what they preach. | |
| 16 | Senior leaders in my organisation are very supportive of new ideas. | |
| 17 | People in my organisation are given time to explore creative ideas and solutions to business challenges and opportunities. | |
| 18 | Leaders in my organisation find the money required to create and implement good ideas. | |
| 19 | People in my organisation are clear on the business challenges or opportunities that require their creative thought. | |
| 20 | People in my organisation are aware of the goals and expectations around creative performance. | |
| | **subtotal** | |

## Organisation-level factors

| | | |
|---|---|---|
| 21 | We are happy to take risks in the pursuit of creating new and breakthrough ideas. | |
| 22 | People in my organisation express their wildest ideas without fear of ridicule. | |
| 23 | There are no disruptive internal politics within my organisation. | |
| 24 | People in my organisation are very supportive of each other. | |
| 25 | Everyone in my organisation is encouraged to participate in innovation. | |
| 26 | There are clear avenues to take in my organisation if I have an idea that I want to take forward. | |
| 27 | The environment I work in is filled with natural light and nature (e.g. pot plants). | |
| 28 | The environment I work in is designed to facilitate collaboration and impromptu meetings with others who may not work in my area. | |
| | subtotal | |

The next step is to tally up your score for items 1 to 6 (individual-level factors), 7 to 12 (team-level factors), 13 to 20 (leader-level factors), and 21 to 28 (organisation-level factors).

## Individual-level factors (*items 1 to 6*)

### *Below average*
*(scores between 1 and 10)*

Your score suggests that there is much room for improvement on the individual-level factors that affect innovation culture. Individuals in your organisation may be low on at least one of the following factors:

*Challenge*. In order for innovation to thrive, people need to feel challenged by the work they do. If people feel they can complete most tasks with their eyes shut, then innovation will be low. If your scores for items 1 and 2 are below 3 on the five-point scale, chapter 1 is a good place to find some ideas about how you can inject more challenges into your own personal work and into the work of your organisation.

*Autonomy*. People with low autonomy may feel micromanaged or feel that they have little choice as to how they complete everyday tasks and projects they are given. If your scores for items 3 and 4 are below 3, chapter 2 will be helpful in providing ways you can start to increase autonomy for yourself and for others within your organisation.

*Recognition*. If you feel like you and others in your organisation are generally not acknowledged for the work that you do, then chances are your scores for items 5 and 6 are below 3. Receiving recognition, at both an individual level and a team or organisation-wide level, is an important driver of innovation culture. If recognition is lacking in your organisation, chapter 3 provides some advice on how you can start to integrate it into what you do.

## Average
*(scores between 11 and 20)*

Chances are that individuals in your organisation feel challenged by their work to a moderate extent, people feel relatively autonomous in how they go about planning their day-to-day work, and some individuals feel recognised for the work they contribute towards innovation. While the good news is that you are not below average, there is still a fair degree of room for improvement.

### Item scores of 3 or below

*Items 1 and 2*. Chapter 1 is a good place to start. This chapter explains how to create more of a sense of challenge for individuals within your organisation. If people don't regularly feel challenged by the work they do, then innovation tends to be dormant.

*Items 3 and 4*. See chapter 2 for advice on how to help individuals feel a greater sense of autonomy over the work they do. If people feel like they don't have freedom over how they do their work, or even what projects they can choose to work on, then you are not giving innovation a chance to thrive.

*Items 5 and 6*. You will benefit from reading chapter 3, which focuses on recognition. Recognising individuals for their innovation efforts is an important factor in motivating people to continue pursuing their ideas.

### Above average
*(scores between 21 and 30)*

Your score suggests that the individual-level factors of challenge, autonomy and recognition are present in your organisation. While this means you could skip ahead to some other chapters, you might want to read chapters 1, 2 and 3 for some advice on how to increase these factors even more.

## Team-level factors (items 7 to 12)

### Below average
*(scores between 1 and 10)*

I recommend focusing your efforts at the team level. Your own team is the best place to start, of course, but all teams within your organisation need to focus on the following three elements to improve innovation culture:

**Debate**. Your score suggests that your team (or other teams in the organisation) do not welcome different points of view. Instead, homogeneity is encouraged and teams in your organisation are probably guilty of a lot of group-think. Chapter 4 explains why debate is so important. It focuses on how to elicit more debate around ideas and provides some practical methods you could use to start improving your performance on this element.

**Team support**. Having a team that is supportive of your and other members' ideas is critical for promoting a culture of innovation. Your score suggests that this support is somewhat absent in your team. Chapter 5 explains how to foster an environment in which team members start to support each other's ideas.

**Collaboration**. Teams within your organisation tend to work in isolation from each other, and collaboration between different teams, departments and the outside world rarely occurs. Chapter 6 focuses on the importance of collaboration and on ways to drive greater collaboration between your team and others within your organisation.

### Average
*(scores between 11 and 20)*

Your team environment is probably somewhat conducive to innovation. There is a fair degree of debate in your team, in that different viewpoints are encouraged; your team is supportive of each others' ideas; and there is a decent amount of collaboration between different teams in your organisation. However, there is still room for your team to be more effective at creating a culture where innovation thrives.

### Item scores of 3 or below

*Items 7 and 8*. See chapter 4 for details on why debate and intellectual stimulation are critical for your team. The chapter explains the problems that arise when team members think in the same way and shun points of view that are different from the mainstream. The chapter also offers practical suggestions of ways to spark more debate within your team.

*Items 9 and 10*. See chapter 5 for a discussion on how you can promote an environment where people in your team are supportive of each other's ideas.

*Items 11 and 12*. See chapter 6 for information on the critical role collaboration plays, and for ideas on how to encourage more collaboration between teams in your organisation.

## Above average
*(scores between 21 and 30)*

Your team, and other teams within your organisation, are probably going very well in regard to being innovative. You might want to skip part II if you are comfortable with the way your team is performing, although you might want to read chapters 4, 5 and 6 for ideas on how to increase these factors even more—for your team, and other teams within the organisation.

## Leader-level factors (*items 13 to 20*)

## Below average
*(scores between 1 and 14)*

Your organisation needs to focus its efforts at the leadership level in order to create a strong culture for innovation. There are four variables that affect innovation culture at the leadership level:

*Supervisor support*. Your scores suggest that supervisors and managers in your organisation are not consistently supportive of innovation. There may be some managers who openly listen to and help push forward ideas, but they tend to be the exception to the rule. Chapter 7 will be helpful for you in understanding how to affect the supportiveness of supervisors and managers when it comes to innovation.

*Senior leader support*. Senior leaders within your organisation may not be particularly supportive of innovation. While this can be a challenging driver to influence (unless you are a senior leader yourself), chapter 8 provides practical examples of how senior leaders at other organisations deliberately encourage innovation across their companies.

*Resourcing*. Your responses suggest that leaders in your organisation do not effectively resource innovation. This may take the form of insufficient money provided for innovation projects, or it may be a lack of time provided for employees to work on innovation. In any case, both types of resources are critical in driving innovation culture. Chapter 9 examines some effective models for how leaders can resource innovation.

*Goal clarity*. Being clear on the goals you are striving for and the challenges you are focused on solving is a significant driver of innovation culture. Your scores suggest that there is a lack of clarity on innovation goals within your organisation. Chapter 10 shows you how to set clear goals and missions for innovation, and the role leaders need to play in setting these goals.

## Average
*(scores between 15 and 25)*

Chances are that leaders within your organisation are moderately skilled at encouraging and fostering innovation. There may be some leaders who are particularly supportive, but on the flip side there may be others who are downright blockers of innovation. If the leaders within your organisation are not all on the same page when it comes to supporting innovation, the leader-level (part III) chapters in this book are good ones for you to read.

### Item scores of 3 or below
*Items 13 and 14*. Chapter 7 could be helpful in explaining the role of supervisor or manager support when it comes to innovation. This chapter explains the role supervisors need to play when it comes to fostering a culture of innovation, and the behaviours they need to display.

*Items 15 and 16.* The amount of senior leader support given to innovation in your organisation could be problematic. Chapter 8 goes into detail about why this factor is so critical, and explains how you can influence senior leaders to become more supportive of innovation.

*Items 17 and 18.* Chances are that innovation is not resourced very effectively where you work. Chapter 9 focuses on how leaders need to resource innovation, specifically looking at the money allocated to innovation and the time people are given to pursue innovation projects.

*Items 19 and 20.* There is room for improvement around the goals being set for innovation. Chapter 10 looks at the importance of setting clear goals and missions for innovation so that employees have a focus and know what is expected of them. This chapter provides practical tips on how leaders can do this.

## Above average
*(scores between 26 and 40)*

Leaders within your organisation are doing a great job at building a culture for innovation. Your score suggests that managers and supervisors across the organisation are very supportive of innovation, and that this continues right up to the top tier of management. In addition, your score suggests that leaders in your organisation resource innovation effectively, in that time and money are given to individuals and teams to pursue innovation projects. Finally, leaders in your company are good at setting clear goals in relation to innovation.

Your high score means that you could skip part III, although if you want to improve your organisation's performance even more around these leader-led elements, see chapters 7, 8, 9 and 10 for practical advice and tips.

## Organisation-level factors (items 21 to 28)

### Below average
*(scores between 1 and 14)*

Focusing your efforts on the organisation-wide drivers of innovation culture will be important for your company. There are four variables that affect innovation culture at the organisation-wide level:

**Risk-taking**. Having a culture where risk-taking is encouraged and where failure is not a dirty word drives innovation. However, this kind of environment is one of the most challenging goals for medium- to large-size organisations to achieve; your score suggests that this environment is not present in your company. Chapter 11 discusses different ways to change your culture so that it is one in which people feel comfortable taking risks.

**Cohesion**. Everyone feeling that they are 'on the same team' and experiencing a strong sense of togetherness is a very significant driver of innovation. Your scores suggest that this is not the case at your company, and that there is considerable conflict between people, teams and departments. Chapter 12 discusses ways in which you can begin to change your environment into one in which relationships are more cohesive across the organisation.

**Participation**. An environment in which individuals feel they have permission (and are indeed actively encouraged) to participate in innovation activities is an important driver of innovation culture. Your score suggests that people are generally not encouraged to come up with ideas and pursue these innovations. Chapter 13 examines why this factor is so important and explains how other organisations create an environment that encourages participation from everyone in the company.

**Physical environment**. The physical office environment in which we work has an enormous effect on innovation. Unfortunately, many offices are not designed with innovation in mind; and, based on your score, it would seem that your organisation fits into this category. Chapter 14 discusses specific ways that you can change and manipulate the physical environment so that it drives a culture of innovation.

## Average
*(scores between 15 and 25)*

Your scores suggest that when it comes to organisation-wide factors, your company's performance overall is moderate. There may be some elements that your organisation is strong at, while others have a lot of room for improvement.

### Item scores of 3 or below

*Items 21 and 22*. Your organisation is not overly comfortable taking risks. Failure and experimentation are not actively encouraged. Chapter 11 provides some tips on improving your organisation's approach and attitude to risk-taking, and offers some practical examples of how other companies are doing this very successfully.

*Items 23 and 24*. There is room for relationships across your organisation to be more cohesive. Having people in your organisation feel an overall sense of togetherness is a very important driver of innovation. Chapter 12 discusses this concept in more detail, and offers practical methods for enhancing your organisation's performance on this variable.

*Items 25 and 26*. People feel somewhat encouraged to participate in innovation and put forward their ideas. Chapter 13 explains ways in which you can actively promote greater participation in innovation from all individuals.

*Items 27 and 28*. The physical environment in your organisation is probably not one that fosters innovation. Chapter 14 provides you with different techniques you can use to enhance your environment so that it actively contributes to driving a culture of innovation.

## Above average
*(scores between 26 and 40)*

Your organisation is performing strongly in several different factors that are important for driving innovation. Your company is very good at encouraging people to take risks, and failure is not stigmatised. Your physical environment is conducive to innovation, and people across the organisation feel a strong sense of togetherness—they feel as if they are all working as part of a big team. Finally, people are actively encouraged to participate in innovation and put forward their ideas. Your high score means that part IV might not be a priority for you, but chapters 11, 12, 13 and 14 outline practical methods for improving innovation at an organisation-wide level.

# PART I

# INDIVIDUAL-LEVEL FACTORS

While many people think of cultural change as something that needs to happen at an organisation-wide level, research has actually revealed that there is much that can be influenced at the individual level—especially when it comes to driving innovation. If you are a manager reading this book, the chapters in this section will provide you with plenty of advice on how to structure tasks and projects in your team, and suggest initiatives that you could consider implementing to help drive a culture of innovation for the individuals in your team.

If you are an individual without direct managerial responsibility, then this section will probably be the most important one you read. The suggestions and ideas contained over the next three chapters are strategies that you will be able to implement readily—for both yourself and your peers.

We start with the challenge of *challenge*. One of the most important factors in creating a strong innovation culture is that individuals need to feel significantly challenged by what they do. Chapter 1 explores what it means to be challenged, what is the 'right' level of challenge to aim for, and gives examples of how other organisations are setting challenges for individuals.

Chapter 2 examines the topic of autonomy. Ensuring people feel a sense of freedom and control over what they do and how they solve problems is a significant driver of innovation. The need to give individuals autonomy in their roles comes up over and over again in the innovation literature. This chapter will provide examples of what it actually means to give autonomy and how to implement these ideas within your organisation.

Providing recognition to individuals is the final individual-level driver that will be explored. Chapter 3 describes what it means to provide recognition and the different ways that organisations can approach this. The chapter will provide you with inspiration and examples of how other organisations approach the topic of recognition, and also answer the question of whether financial rewards actually serve as an effective motivator of innovation.

# CHAPTER 1

# CHALLENGE

## The Goldilocks factor—finding the level that's just right

Jeff Immelt took over from Jack Welch as the CEO of General Electric (GE) on Friday 7 September 2001, four days before two planes flew into the World Trade Center towers. It is an understatement to say that his timing was rough. Welch had delivered GE's shareholders average returns of 23 per cent per annum during his two decades as the company's leader. Welch's success had come from clever acquisitions and improving efficiencies, but Immelt felt he needed to take a different tack. In his first two years he focused on investments in R&D and leadership and on identifying new growth opportunities for the business. However, by the end of his second year, income and revenue were at levels similar to where they were back in 2000.

Immelt knew he had to go even further in his pursuit of organic growth. He created an initiative that is still front and centre at GE today. Immelt brought together his top marketing directors from across GE's varying businesses in September 2003 and asked them each to develop five Imagination Breakthroughs. These were defined as new business proposals that would deliver new growth to GE.

And they had to be delivered within two months. In November 2003, 50 Imagination Breakthroughs were presented to Immelt and 35 were green-lighted.

Imagination Breakthroughs (or IBs, as they are called within the organisation) are now a core part of business leaders' roles at GE. Every year leaders are challenged to come up with three IBs, which are defined as new projects that can deliver $100 million of incremental growth within three years.

IBs are incredibly high-profile at GE. If you are asked to work on or contribute to an IB project, you re-prioritise everything else to accommodate it. This means that while the leaders feel a huge sense of challenge in presenting three IBs each year, they also have the resources at their disposal to rise up to and meet the challenge.

Within five years of the program's inception, IBs had generated $3 billion in incremental revenues for GE, and the company had hit its growth targets for 14 continuous quarters.

★★★

It's important to feel challenged by your work, and this is borne out by many studies that link challenge to increased creativity and innovation. In the 2007 meta-analysis 'Climate for creativity: A quantitative review', Samuel Hunter and his colleagues found that employees feeling a strong sense of challenge in their work is one of the strongest drivers of a culture of innovation. They defined challenge as the 'perception that jobs and/or tasks are challenging, complex and interesting—yet at the same time not overly taxing or unduly overwhelming'. It is important that you don't simply think about how to give people the biggest possible challenge. Instead you should ensure that the level of challenge you set is one that is achievable. On the flip side, setting tasks that people are able to complete with their eyes closed will not breed a culture where innovation thrives.

So why is challenge so necessary for innovation? The answer lies in the work of Mihaly Csikszentmihalyi, a professor of psychology and management at Claremont Graduate University. Csikszentmihalyi is best-known for researching a concept called 'flow'. Flow, or 'being in the zone', is the state of complete absorption in a task. If you have ever been working intensely on a project and suddenly realised that an hour, or several, have flown by, you were probably in a state of flow.

In a nutshell, there are two preconditions for flow. The first one is a high degree of skill in the task you are doing. The second precondition is challenge—that is, working on a task that you would define as challenging or difficult. Csikszentmihalyi found that employees experience flow 44 per cent of the time, and experience boredom 20 per cent of the time. The rest of the time—36 per cent—is filled with anxiety. Finding tasks and projects that challenge you (or your team) will help to increase the percentage of time spent in flow—just so long as you have the skills and abilities to rise to the challenge. If you don't, it will simply result in increased anxiety.

> If you have ever been working intensely on a project and suddenly realised that an hour, or several, have flown by, you were probably in a state of flow.

GE's Imagination Breakthrough program is a great example of how to ensure people feel an optimal level of challenge. The challenge set is a big one—finding new business ideas that will contribute $100 million of incremental growth—but leaders are given an entire year to develop three new growth ideas. The challenge is big, but the resources made available to leaders make it a challenge that they can meet.

★★★

The U-shaped relationship between challenge and performance —or, more specifically, innovation—has long been recognised by academics and researchers. Back in 1908, a couple of psychologists, Robert Yerkes and John Dodson, published a paper that challenged the way people thought about mental arousal and performance. They found that a high level of arousal enhances performance on simple tasks. That is, it is a simple linear relationship: the more alert and focused people are, the better their performance. However, they found that a high level of arousal actually decreases performance on complex tasks. In fact what they found was that an intermediate level of arousal was best for task performance. This 'inverted U' relationship became known as the Yerkes–Dodson law (see figure 1.1).

**Figure 1.1:** Yerkes–Dodson law

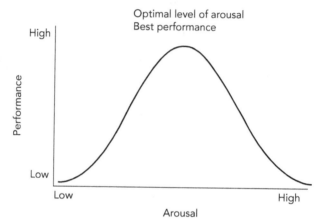

Surprisingly, the Yerkes–Dodson law is often misinterpreted by researchers and members of the public alike. Many people completely ignore the very important finding that the inverted U-shape applies only to complex tasks — not simple ones. For simpler tasks, the U-shaped curve is much flatter, as we can deal with a greater range of arousal when completing basic tasks such as brushing our teeth.

This brings us to the topic of how the Yerkes–Dodson law applies to innovation. One of the things that characterises an innovation project or challenge is that it is far from simple. If it were simple, many other companies would have already cracked the problem and moved on. Instead, projects requiring innovation are always complex. So it is critical that innovation projects are matched with people who have the appropriate skill sets for the task, and that those people also have the resources available to rise to the challenge.

At Circus Oz, Australia's leading international circus troupe, Artistic Director and joint CEO Mike Finch describes having a sense of challenge as being built into the DNA of the art form. 'Every single action is a challenge—and quite often, life-threatening. If you lose concentration, you can't achieve it. It's a challenge even just to do the most basic act that you've done for ten years.'

While rising to the challenge is somewhat easier in front of 'Doctor Footlights', as live performance is referred to by the team, the sense of challenge can be harder to foster during the long rehearsal period between shows. One of the ways Finch tries to encourage his team to challenge themselves and to be disruptive is to find a skill they can do really well, and ask them to change one element of it.

'We had a performer called Michael Ling', says Finch, 'who was with the company for 28 years as a performer. One of the skills he had was going up a sway-pole, which is a 6-metre tall, bendy steel pole. One of the things we used to do is dress the pole like a lamppost and have his character, a cleaner, climb to the top to clean the post. He would then do a handstand on top and the whole thing would sway left to right and front and back. He'd lean out over the audience.

'Michael also had another character he developed which was an elderly man. Michael was in his forties, but he could jump instantly from being a boy to being an 80-year-old character. Both of these characters and skills were right in his comfort zone.

'One of the ways we challenged him was by getting him to put these two completely disparate things together.

*(continued)*

I asked, "What would the old man be like up on the sway-pole?" So with this challenge in mind, Ling created something completely different.'

This challenge resulted in the stunning final act of the season they were in rehearsals for. Ling had established himself as the old man, in a wheelchair on the ground. Thanks to some clever illusions, he was suddenly transported to the top of a sway-pole (which was dressed as a palm tree), on his wheelchair. 'There was a whole lot of disruption but it was him on top of this tall pole and playing this old man and finding a brand-new way to put those two things together. All this brand-new material came from asking, "What does a geriatric do when they're 6 metres up in the air, swaying around and on a wheelchair?"

'For me, challenge is not taking people so far out of their comfort zone that they're terrified', says Finch. 'It can actually be just doing something you already know well, but doing it in a completely different way.'

★★★

There is a lot of research to support the relationship between individuals having challenging work and producing significantly more innovative outcomes. In their study 'Assessing the work environment for creativity', Professor Teresa Amabile, from Harvard University, and her colleagues investigated the impact of challenging work on a group of middle managers working at a large American electronics company. The study first required each manager to nominate their 'highest creativity' project from the last three years, and also their 'lowest creativity' project. Managers were instructed to choose only projects where creativity was the desired outcome. This process led to a total of 306 projects being nominated, and each project was then assessed by an independent judge to validate that it was indeed a creative or non-creative outcome.

The final stage of the study involved finding people who had worked on these projects and asking them about their experiences. One of the questions asked team members how challenging they found the project in terms of the work they were asked to contribute. Amabile and her colleagues found that those working on projects with a creative outcome were significantly more likely to have felt a strong sense of challenge in the work that they did. Indeed, challenging work was one of the biggest differentiators between creative and non-creative project outcomes.

In another study, conducted by Amabile and Dr Stanley Gryszkiewicz, 120 R&D scientists were interviewed with the view to understanding what drives innovation in their work environment. The R&D scientists were asked to describe two events: one that exemplified a project that produced highly innovative outcomes, and another that did not. They were then asked to describe the characteristics of the environment and the people working on the projects in as much detail as possible.

After analysing the transcripts, Amabile and Gryszkiewicz found some very big differences between the projects. Many of the scientists spoke about the sense of challenge that was present for the highly innovative projects. For example, one scientist said, 'We were put in a situation where we were told it couldn't be done; other companies had turned down the offer ... So there was a challenge. That challenge gave us our motivation'.

Another finding from the research around this sense of challenge was that it was not driven so much by external pressure, but was intrinsically generated. One scientist commented, 'This was not something that was imposed on them, but a problem that they generated themselves. There were no specific deadlines, but a sense of urgency that was internalized'. Another participant described it further as, 'The marketplace is competitive and therefore we feel compelled to compete'.

The researchers concluded that having a positive sense of pressure is a very important driver of innovation, and of project teams producing creative outcomes. And, more specifically, if the sense of pressure can be generated from within the individual, then it becomes a far more motivating force.

★★★

Professor Greg Oldham and his colleague Anne Cummings from the University of Illinois set out to explore the impact of having a challenging job on creative performance. One hundred and seventy-one employees from two manufacturing facilities participated in the research. There were participants from a variety of job areas, including design engineers, manufacturing engineers, design drafters, toolmakers and technicians. While employees were asked questions about their work and their role, their supervisors were asked to describe the employee's creative output. Specifically, they were asked how innovative the employee's work output was; how many patent disclosures they had written; and whether any suggestions the employee had made to an internal suggestion program had been accepted by the organisation over a two-year period.

Oldham found that there was a significant relationship between employees feeling challenged by their work and the complexity of their tasks, and creative output as rated by their supervisor. Oldham also found that when participants who possessed characteristics that are more commonly associated with creative people (for example, being individualistic, unconventional and reflective) experienced a sense of challenge, it led to an increase in the number of suggestions submitted to the internal innovation program.

> ...if people are in a role that challenges them, 67 per cent will demonstrate above-average creativity and innovation in their performance.

In a 2014 review of several meta-analyses, Silvia da Costa, from the University of the Basque Country, and several of her colleagues examined the difference in creativity for those in challenging versus non-challenging roles. The researchers found that if people are in a role that challenges them, 67 per cent will demonstrate above-average creativity and innovation in their performance. In contrast, only 33 per cent of people in 'easy' jobs show above-average innovativeness.

★★★

The notion of challenging work leading to increased innovation is not surprising to most people. What is surprising is how little consideration is given to appropriately and deliberately matching the challenge or task complexity to the individual person. When most managers allocate tasks to their team, the primary question considered is whether the person has capacity. Obviously, capacity is relevant. However, in addition to considering capacity (or 'time'), managers need to give more conscious thought to how challenged the person will feel about certain tasks, and allocate accordingly.

When new work comes in at Inventium I always take time to consider who in my team will feel stretched by the work. Obviously, there will be instances where I'll need to allocate work to people who will find a project relatively straightforward, especially on occasions when those who would feel challenged by the project are already at full capacity. But sense of challenge always comes into the equation when assigning projects to people. Another element we consider at Inventium is how much time our innovation consultants are allocated to client work versus professional development activities. We try to ensure that no-one spends more than three days per week on client work, which leaves about one day a week for business development and the rest of the time for development activities—which generally involves either learning or creating new intellectual property (which is inevitably a challenging part of the role). In addition, my team recently created a monthly initiative called PD (personal development) Hacks. Once a month we go off-site, sit together in a new environment and each work on development activities. (Last month we went to work at a local museum.)

If you are not in a managerial position—or even if you are—take time regularly to reflect on how challenged you feel by the tasks and projects you are working on. If you feel that the majority of projects you are given are ones you could complete with your hands tied behind your back, then have a chat to your manager about being given some more challenging and complex work. Likewise, if you feel that the work you are being set is causing you too much stress because you lack either the skills or resources to do a great job, this should also act as a trigger. Speak to your manager about setting more realistic challenges as part of your role.

# KEY POINTS

- Matching the level of challenge to an individual's skill level is key to finding the optimal level of challenge and getting into a state of flow.

- When setting challenges for your team ensure they have the resources available to meet those challenges. If they don't, the challenges will create more stress than innovation.

- As a manager, take time to thoughtfully consider how you allocate tasks and projects to people. Ensure that you are matching these elements so that people feel a significant sense of challenge.

- If your manager is not providing you with enough challenge (or, on the flip side, if they're providing you with too much)—speak up! Work together to find the optimal balance.

# CHAPTER 2

# AUTONOMY

## Should you loosen the reins?

Imagine you work as a developer for Etsy. In case you haven't heard of Etsy, it is a marketplace where people around the world connect, both online and offline, to make, sell and buy unique goods. It has 1.5 million sellers, almost 22 million active buyers, and in 2014 it had gross merchandise sales of almost $2 billion. So you could say it's doing quite well.

Now let's just say you happen to notice a problem with the Etsy website, or perhaps you think of a way it could be improved. At most organisations you would probably tell your manager about the problem, who would probably tell his or her manager, and after waiting a few weeks you might then get approval to make your desired change. In short, you have very limited ability to make changes you believe are important.

At Etsy it's a completely different story. When I met up with Chad Dickerson, Etsy's CEO and chairman, in their Brooklyn offices in New York, he told me that anyone in the team can make a change to the Etsy website whenever they see a need. (Etsy.com had over 40 million unique views per month when we spoke; at the time of writing it has around 60 million.)

'We do something on the engineering team called continuous deployment', explains Dickerson. 'That's a fancy way of saying that we've given every software developer, every product manager the ability to change the site at any time. Back in 2009 when we started this approach, not many companies were doing this. Typically, websites do a release every two weeks. We release or do code deploys about 35 times a day [this has since increased to up to 50 times per day]. The really exciting thing is that there's no central authority that manages the releases.'

In practice, the developers at Etsy manage the releases with each other. 'If I'm a developer and I'm making a change to the site, I get into what's called a push queue. I tell everyone else that I'm about to push code and it's almost like the whole neighbourhood is watching you', says Dickerson.

Every single person at Etsy has the ability to do this without explicit approval. It's very, very decentralised and very, very fast. And if you ever go for a tour around Etsy's head office in Brooklyn, you will see monitors with all kinds of charts and graphs showing how many code deploys they have done in a day.

Through continuous deployment, the team at Etsy is always experimenting and gathering data. 'We are able to push things out and test, push things out, test, push things out, test, on a really rapid basis', says Dickerson. 'We're able to learn about products and make changes for the better pretty much constantly. If you have a two-week release cycle, you can only learn new things every two weeks. In our case, you learn something new every 20 minutes, which is really exciting.'

One final key benefit of continuous deployment is that the approach has a bias towards action. In an organisation where releases are done only every couple of weeks, or every month or so, it becomes so easy for someone to suggest improvements and for that suggestion to get lost in the noise. 'I think when you can deploy code at any time and make a change at any time, it makes it a lot harder to say "We should do this", because the answer is: just do it', says Dickerson.

By giving everyone in the organisation the power to make real change, innovation is dramatically enhanced. You might be thinking, 'There is no way I would trust my team to make changes to a website that is getting 40 million unique views a month'. But think about it from an Etsy developer's point of view. There is no way they are going to make a change without feeling very confident it will make the website better, because all eyes are on them.

Etsy certainly isn't the only large web-based organisation that encourages continuous deployment. Vimeo, one of the world's largest video-sharing websites, has exactly the same policy. Any given day will see over 30 changes deployed to Vimeo.com.

'You can't keep track of all the pushes that go on because they're constantly fixing, they're constantly upgrading. We just try not to do things on Friday afternoons!' says Dae Mellencamp, Vimeo's president.

The essence of continuous deployment is that it grants employees autonomy over their work. People have the freedom to fix things that need fixing, and make improvements where they see fit. Continuous deployment doesn't require managerial approval, nor does it involve a manager simply telling an employee what to do.

> By giving everyone in the organisation the power to make real change, innovation is dramatically enhanced.

★★★

Many researchers have found that creativity is dramatically enhanced when employees are given the freedom to decide how they do their jobs. When people feel as if they have a choice in how things can be done they are significantly more likely to engage in trial and error and, through this, find more effective ways of doing things.

If you work in a web-based business such as Etsy or Vimeo it's a straightforward idea to implement, but it can be slightly more challenging to apply if you work in, say, manufacturing. The trick to applying continuous deployment is to think about what the principle means at its core. Essentially it means giving employees the freedom to make significant changes that will be experienced by customers (whether these be internal or external) without first being given approval by management.

This might, for example, involve giving employees the freedom to make changes to internal processes. It might involve making changes to company initiatives. It's worth thinking about what your organisation's version of continuous deployment might look like. At Circus Oz, Artistic Director and joint-CEO Mike Finch describes any performance season as being in a state of continuous deployment. 'Essentially we're doing a software update every night and at several different points in the show. The fabulous thing about circus is you have a focus group that is actually responding live to every product "shipment".'

During performance seasons, once or sometimes twice a day, the troupe will sit down together and receive 20 minutes of notes from the director. 'Sometimes it's really pragmatic', explains Finch. 'Like "we have to cut that bit tonight so the rigger needs to know to tie that knot at the right time", but once it settles in, you get this really great flow state where we are able to play around as a group. We will often spend the time asking the ensemble, "Let's try something new!" — like — what if we all leaned in a different direction at this point? You might just do a ten- or 15-minute rehearsal with the whole group, and everyone will suggest ways to improve the show and experiment with different ideas.

Over time, if you have the same ensemble and the same basic structure, the show gets tighter and tighter and more effective and funnier and more interesting and richer in layers.'

Etsy, Vimeo and Circus Oz are examples of companies that have embraced the concept of giving employees a significant degree of autonomy. And providing autonomy to individuals is a critical driver of an innovation culture.

★★★

Autonomy is giving people choice instead of telling them what to do. In 'How to kill creativity' Harvard professor Teresa Amabile describes it as:

> giving people … the means — that is, concerning process — but not necessarily the ends. People will be more creative, in other words, if you give them freedom to decide how to climb a particular mountain. You needn't let them choose which mountain to climb. In fact, clearly specified strategic goals often enhance people's creativity.

There has been a great deal of research on the impact of autonomy on creative performance right through from childhood to working adulthood. What it has found is that not only does autonomy drive innovation in adults, but the effect has also been seen in children as young as two or three years of age.

In one such study, Amabile and her colleague Judith Gitomer set out to explore the effect of task autonomy in preschoolers aged between two and six years old. They separated the children into two groups. Both groups were asked to create their own collage — with one critical difference. The first group of children were given the ability to choose any type of materials they wanted, while the second group were given a pre-determined set of materials — that is, they had no choice. Professional artists were then brought in to judge the creativeness of each collage. Collages created by children in the first group were judged to be significantly more creative. Amabile and Gitomer concluded that the freedom given to children to select their own materials contributed to their collages being judged to be the most creative.

When it comes to adults, there are many studies showing a clear relationship between autonomy and creative performance. For example, Diana Krause's 2004 study of several organisations in Germany examined the effects of granting autonomy on the behaviour of 399 mid-level managers. Krause discovered that employees who were given a high level of freedom in choosing how to complete tasks generated and prototyped significantly more ideas than employees who were given little autonomy.

In another study, Dr Carolyn Axtell, a psychologist from the University of Sheffield, and her colleagues examined 148 machine operators who all worked for a beverage company in the north of England. The researchers asked these employees how much control they felt they had over their role and how they approached tasks, as well as questions about the types of new ideas and process improvements they had suggested and implemented. While autonomy didn't have an impact on the implementation of ideas, it had a significant impact on the number of ideas suggested by the machine operators—in that the more freedom the operator had, the more ideas and improvements they were likely to suggest to their team and manager.

★★★

Professor Ellen Greenberg from the University of Massachusetts was interested in the effect of autonomy on creative workers—specifically, fashion designers. Greenberg's study involved 96 fashion students from the United States who were given different levels of choice with regard to making a dress for a formal occasion. Some students were told who they would be designing a dress for (for example, the Queen), while others were able to choose from a long list of women. In addition to being given choice over who they were designing the dress for, some students were given flexibility over their deadline, and some were supervised more closely than others.

> …what is most important about autonomy is having freedom in the actual task, as opposed to the timing of the task or how involved one's manager is.

All the dresses were assessed for creativity by a panel of three fashion professionals. In line with Greenberg's hypothesis, students who were able to choose the woman for whom they were designing the dress produced significantly more creative dresses. However, somewhat surprisingly, a student's ability to choose their deadline did not affect creative output, and neither did having a more 'obtrusive' supervisor. This study highlights the fact that what is most important about autonomy is having freedom in the actual task, as opposed to the timing of the task or how involved one's manager is.

Silvia da Costa, from the University of the Basque Country, and several of her colleagues examined the difference in innovation performance for those in roles where autonomy was high, versus roles where it was low. The researchers found that 63 per cent of people in a highly autonomous role will demonstrate above-average creativity and innovation in their performance. In contrast, only 37 per cent of people in jobs with little freedom show above-average innovativeness.

The more experience you have with being given autonomy in performing tasks, the greater the creative performance resulting from the autonomy will be. Jin Wook Chang, from Carnegie Mellon University, and his colleagues examined this notion with a group of 148 South Korean university students. Students were divided into two groups and invited to undergo three creative problem-solving tasks in the lab. Group 1 was given freedom to decide how long they spent on each task, and had permission to chop and change between tasks. Group 2 was instructed to spend a set amount of time working on each task and to move sequentially through the three tasks. Chang and his colleagues found that students who had been given autonomy previously performed significantly more creatively in the first condition—when given autonomy with the creative problem-solving tasks. However, those who had not been given significant freedom in the past did not exhibit the same increase in creative performance on tasks when they were given autonomy. The lesson for managers is that if you have not given your team a lot of freedom in the past, then don't expect an instant result when you do start to provide autonomy. People need to experience autonomy and gain confidence in their choices through experience before they start to show a significant increase in their creativity.

★★★

It's not just innovation performance that benefits from autonomy; studies demonstrate that autonomy has positive effects on general performance, too. Richard Locke, a professor of entrepreneurship at MIT, and his colleagues conducted one such study that compared performance across two Mexican factories that both made t-shirts for Nike. The factories were similar in that they both provided the same kinds of products to Nike and operated according to the same codes of conduct. But in other ways the factories were dramatically different, both in terms of how they operated and in their productivity and output.

At Plant A, employees were given a lot of freedom and autonomy. Employees were asked to contribute their opinions to all sorts of issues, ranging from production targets to scheduling and operations. The decision to work overtime was given to the employees, not made for them; and the workplace was very collaborative. In contrast, Plant B was very hierarchical and orders were dictated from the top. Employees had very little freedom, and overtime was forced, not voluntary.

While employee satisfaction was, not surprisingly, significantly higher at Plant A, the differences in production output were even more striking. The average labour cost to produce a t-shirt at Plant B was 18 cents, while at Plant A the cost per t-shirt was 11 cents—around 40 per cent lower. In addition, employees at Plant A each produced an average of 150 t-shirts per day, compared with only 80 t-shirts per day at Plant B.

At Inventium I take special care to give my team autonomy. However, letting others decide how best to approach a task is not something that comes naturally to me. I am a perfectionist by nature, and perfectionists are not good at delegating or providing autonomy to others (because in their mind, no-one will ever do as good a job as they will).

Recruiting the right people has been key to me providing my team with freedom. I always try to recruit people who are smarter than me on several dimensions. For example, two of the women on my team have MBAs from a couple of the world's top business schools, and we also recently recruited someone who has a Masters in Economics. I know that if I set these people a project in their areas of expertise—around business strategy or operations, for example—they will do a far better job than I would. Which makes it easy to give autonomy.

We recently recruited an ex-Apple employee who has been invaluable in improving all things digital within Inventium (not to mention fixing my MacBook Air several times in the past few months). It is much harder for managers to grant the necessary freedom to people in their jobs if they don't fundamentally trust their people or believe that their people are smarter or more capable than them in some way, shape or form.

There are several ways in which managers can mismanage autonomy. Firstly, some managers fail to define clear goals for their people. There is much research showing that autonomy on its own is not enough to drive innovation. If people don't know what they should be aiming for, then all the freedom in the world won't help them be more creative. Essentially, freedom becomes pointless unless clear goals and strategies are set. (See chapter 10 for advice on ensuring that people are clear on their overall goals and missions.) Once you have ensured that people know what they should be aiming for, you can give them freedom to work out how best to get there.

> In the absence of clear goals, autonomy is fairly useless.

A second mistake managers make when it comes to managing for autonomy is that they change the goalposts. Imagine that you have been set a goal, and have been given the freedom to decide how you work towards achieving that goal. But then the goal changes midway through the process. This causes huge frustration. Shifting goalposts can often render the work a person has done useless, thus undermining the benefits of autonomy.

Finally, some managers pay lip-service to autonomy. They say they give their employees freedom, when in fact they have prescribed the process that employees need to follow in order to achieve the goals they have been set. If you have a manager who does this, you might want to politely draw their attention to this paradox, because it is counterproductive to innovative work.

If you happen to be a manager reading this book, hopefully the antidotes to the problems mentioned here are obvious. Firstly, you need to ensure that you set clear goals for all individuals in your team. In the absence of clear goals, autonomy is fairly useless. Secondly, you need to ensure that you don't move the goalposts. Doing so will only lead to frustration, no matter how much freedom you give your team. And finally, don't fall into the trap of saying you give people freedom if in reality you dictate how every project and task should be executed.

★★★

As mentioned, one of the best ways to enhance the benefits of autonomy is to give people a clear goal. The goal acts as a focal point, to counterbalance the autonomy, which research has shown to be very important in driving innovation.

At Etsy, one of the ways success is measured is through gross merchandise sales — which is the dollar value of items sold on its marketplace. Dickerson explains, 'We feel like when sellers are selling then that's an indication that things are going pretty well.

'What I've done is basically set targets for that number. We have about 15 or 16 different teams inside Etsy — I tell them what that target is and then I don't really give them any guidance on how to meet that target. What I found is giving people really clear goals but not telling them specifically what to do means they come up with their own plans and they feel more invested in those plans.'

Netflix's CEO, Reed Hastings, states the importance of managers setting context but not control. Hastings describes context as ensuring that employees are clear on the strategy and objectives, and how success will be measured. Clearly defined roles and transparent decision-making also provide clear context. And rather than blame employees when something goes wrong, he suggests that managers first need to ask themselves 'What context did you fail to set?'

Rather than thinking about autonomy and freedom solely in the context of work tasks and projects, another way to provide autonomy and display trust is through company policies. There has been a recent trend towards companies doing away with traditional vacation policies, and instead allowing employees to take whatever they feel they need. Netflix is one company that has opted to move in this direction.

Hastings shared this policy with the world in a presentation uploaded to SlideShare that attracted over 11 million views. Among other things, the presentation covers the huge degree of freedom Netflix employees are given. In the presentation, Hastings says, 'Our model is to increase employee freedom as we grow, rather than limit it, to continue to attract and nourish innovative people, so we have a better chance of sustained success'. But what proved to be most controversial was the revelation that Netflix, a company with over $5 billion in annual revenue and more than 2000 employees, doesn't track annual leave. There is no vacation policy. You simply take what you need. Likewise, unlike many large companies that have complex policies around employee spending and reimbursements, Netflix simplifies its policy to one simple sentence: 'Act in Netflix's best interests'.

★★★

But what if you are an employee who is falling victim to a manager who fails to give you freedom? You may be reading this and thinking, 'There is no way my manager is going to grant me more freedom to do my work. My manager has and always will be a micromanager'. The good news is — there is still hope for you!

Chantal Levesque, a professor of education psychology, and her colleague Luc Pelletier, wanted to explore whether a sense of freedom could be manufactured — even in the presence of a dreaded micromanager. Levesque and Pelletier invited people to their lab and divided them into two groups. The first group was asked to read several sentences, which included words related to the concept of obligation and a lack of autonomy, such as 'forced', 'pressured' and 'controlled'. A second group was asked to read sentences containing words that related to autonomy and freedom, such as 'absorbed', 'interested', 'delighted' and 'challenge'. The aim of reading these words was to prime participants into feeling a sense of autonomy — or lack thereof, in the case of the first group.

Levesque and Pelletier found a very significant difference between the two groups. People who were primed to feel autonomous — by reading sentences about autonomy — felt significantly more engaged in a task they had to complete after reading the sentences. In contrast, the group that read sentences about obligation felt substantially less motivated to complete the task. This study shows that if you are unlucky enough to have a manager who doesn't give you the freedom to choose how you do your work, you can still get yourself into the same zone that real autonomy provides by reading words or stories about autonomy.

One final take on autonomy comes from *Work Rules!* by Google's vice president of people operations, Laszlo Bock. Bock writes that one of the guiding principles of Google's culture is that everyone is encouraged to 'act like a Founder'. He says that in any organisation, in any role, people have a fundamental choice — they can either act like an employee or they can act like a founder. Note that this doesn't necessarily mean acting like the founder of the company — it might mean acting like the founder of their team, or of a project, for example. But fundamentally, it involves people taking responsibility for their environment — in other words, rather than waiting to be given autonomy, taking it for themselves. And when there's a combination of acting like a founder and acting in the best interests of the company (like Netflix encourages its employees to do), great things can happen.

# KEY POINTS

- Give employees the freedom to decide how they do their jobs and complete tasks.

- Ensure that you set clear goals when giving people freedom and autonomy. As a result, performance will significantly improve.

- Recruit people who are smarter than you in some way. It makes it easier to give them freedom to choose how they go about completing tasks and projects.

- Consider how you can use company policies to signal and provide people with more autonomy.

- Think about what your organisation's version of continuous deployment is. How can you provide your team with permission to make changes that will directly affect the customer without first getting approval from management?

- And if all else fails and you happen to be in a situation where you are given very little freedom to do your job, you can artificially boost your sense of autonomy just by taking a few minutes to focus your thoughts on the concepts of freedom and autonomy.

# CHAPTER 3

# RECOGNITION

Money or medals, which works best?

If you love good recommendations on places to eat, drink and visit, chances are you have probably used Foursquare at some point in time. Foursquare is a mobile app company that started in 2009 and aims to help over 45 million users find great places to go, based on their current location. Foursquare's New York offices look exactly like what you would expect from one of the most successful mobile app companies on the planet. Exposed beams, polished floorboards and long communal tables abound. There is also a timeline of Foursquare's journey on a blackboard wall (right behind a table-tennis table, of course), which details all the major milestones in the company's short history. The conference rooms are all named after the badges that users can 'achieve' on Foursquare. And a couple of London-style phone booths are available for those who want some privacy for a phone call.

Evan Cohen was chief operating officer at Foursquare for the bulk of its rise to fame (from 2010 until 2014) as one of New York's most successful start-ups. It now has around 200 employees and it's hard to think of it as a start-up anymore. At Foursquare, recognition is a really important part of how they create a culture where people just love to innovate.

'Every second Friday is engineer demo day', explains Cohen. 'We have a meeting in the main room, and even though it's just for the engineers to present, a lot of other people come too. The engineers plug their laptops into big screens and they show their colleagues what they've been working on. It's about work in progress, not, "Hey this thing shipped".'

And while we traditionally think about recognition in terms of something managers should be providing, at Foursquare peer recognition is just as important. 'They are really fun and interesting sessions but I think there's a lot of subtle peer pressure to show something pretty cool and dazzle people. The engineers love it when they can get people excited and show how what they are working on is cooler than what it was two weeks ago. And forget what your boss thinks, here's 40 of your peers looking! Despite the peer pressure, it is a genuinely supportive environment.'

American-based software company Intuit takes recognition for innovation very seriously. The company has created several different types of innovation awards to recognise employees who have produced brilliant innovations. The pinnacle of Intuit's innovation awards, the Founder's Innovation Award, is presented by Intuit's founder, Scott Cook, and CEO Brad Smith. The Founder's Innovation Award is $1 million (half given in cash and the other half in stock). The award exists to recognise employees who have made an outstanding contribution to the company's growth. And while this award obviously involves a huge cash prize, the prestige and recognition factor is enormous.

Hugh Molotsi, vice president of Intuit Labs Incubator, received the award in 2011 for work he had done in creating and growing Intuit's Payment Solutions business, which now delivers around $100 million in revenue annually.

As well as the Founder's Innovation Award, which is given out 'as warranted', there are also the Scott Cook Innovation Awards, which are annual. They are presented by Scott Cook at an annual leadership conference that has a company-wide audience. The awards recognise teams that have delivered an innovation that is new to the company and has demonstrated a benefit to one of Intuit's three stakeholder groups: employees, customers or shareholders.

'If somebody has built something, and it's been launched into market and has customers using it, then it becomes eligible for an innovation award', explains Molotsi. 'Similarly, if somebody builds something that improves an internal process that's making employees more efficient, that could also become eligible.

'Right now, as we speak, there is a nomination process going on, because they solicit nominations from around the company. Anybody can nominate somebody. They have a vetting process and then they'll typically hand out between five and fifteen of these innovation awards. That's a pretty big deal because it's very prestigious. It's company-wide recognition.'

Winners receive a spot on the Innovation Wall of Fame, dinner with the executive team and an expenses-paid three-day trip anywhere in the continental United States. But in addition to the prizes, they are also given up to three months to dedicate to working on an innovation project of their choice.

✱✱✱

Recognition has long been known to be an important driver of employee engagement, but it is also a very important factor in creating a culture where innovation thrives. To understand why recognition and rewards — and more importantly, why specific types of recognition and rewards — are so powerful when it comes to driving innovation, a couple of core concepts from psychology come into play: intrinsic and extrinsic motivation.

Extrinsic motivation occurs when people engage in behaviours simply because of an external consequence that will come from behaving in a certain way. For example, an individual might work extra hard in the month leading up to pay reviews, because they know that by doing so they are more likely to receive a pay rise.

Intrinsic motivation is in place when people engage in a behaviour or activity because of an internal driver — for enjoyment or satisfaction, for example. When individuals are intrinsically motivated, the motivation and thus their behaviours tend to be significantly more enduring than when they are extrinsically motivated. The main problem with extrinsic motivation is that as soon as the consequence or reward is taken away, motivation disappears.

Back in the 1960s it was thought that these two types of motivation worked together and were additive — in that an increase in one would promote an increase in the other. However, what we now know, largely through the work of Edward Deci, a professor of psychology at the University of Rochester, is that extrinsic rewards can actually reduce intrinsic motivation, specifically when those extrinsic rewards reduce an individual's levels of choice and autonomy. The big exception to this rule is that positive evaluation of performance, or recognition, actually increases intrinsic motivation.

When it comes to innovation, organisations tend to 'reward' performance in two primary ways: by providing recognition, whether publicly through company-wide awards programs or more privately through manager–employee conversations; and by providing financial incentives.

Much research has focused on the effects of both types of reward and on discovering which is most effective for a), increasing individuals' motivation to innovate and b), contributing to a culture of innovation. Researchers such as Professor Teresa Amabile have repeatedly found that recognition plays an important role in driving innovation. Public or private recognition has been shown to significantly improve the level of innovativeness in people's work output, in addition to strengthening the perception of the organisation having a culture that supports innovation. Financial rewards can be part of that support and recognition (explained later in this chapter) but simple recognition is the more powerful motivator.

> Public or private recognition has been shown to significantly improve the level of innovativeness in people's work output.

★★★

Coca-Cola Amatil, one of the world's top five bottlers of Coca-Cola, has an annual awards ceremony for innovation. Anyone in the organisation can nominate an innovation for an Innov8 Award (which is named after the company's innovation program). The awards are incredibly prestigious and have had an enormous impact in providing recognition to those who have done amazing things within the company.

Derek O'Donnell, creator and leader of the Innov8 program, remembers just how big an impact the awards had, even in their first year, on one of the award-winning employees. This particular employee worked in Coca-Cola Amatil's Northmead manufacturing plant and was of Indian heritage. He was in his mid 50s at the time and came to the awards dressed immaculately in a beautiful suit and wearing a turban. 'He came up to me at the end of the night. He had won an award and there were tears flowing down his face. He said to me, "I just want to thank you". I told him, "Oh, no. You don't need to thank me. You're the one who actually won the award". He replied, "No, you don't understand. My children [who at the time were 17 and 19] have always been the ones to come home with awards. All through their school journey, they have come home with different trophies and certificates and I have been so proud as their father. This is the first time I'm going to go home and as their father, be able to say I've won an award".'

O'Donnell remembers being so excited for the employee that he called him the following day. 'I said, "How did you go with your family last night?" He said, "Well, I got home. It was a bit after midnight. I woke the kids up, and we celebrated, and we all went to bed at half four".

'I was struck by the fact that he is actually very introverted, a quiet man who has worked in the organisation for around 25 years. He had great ideas, but wasn't very confident in expressing them. The Innov8 program and awards allowed his voice to be heard and acknowledged. The pride factor for him was huge.'

Another way that Coca-Cola Amatil provides recognition for great ideas is through an initiative called Innov8 Hours. Innov8 Hours provides the opportunity for individuals or teams who have been working on innovations to present their work to others in the organisation in five- or ten-minute chunks. A typical Innov8 Hour is introduced by a senior leader from the organisation who speaks about why innovation is so important for Coca-Cola Amatil. This is then followed by several short presentations by innovation teams and then time for some discussion around innovation. Innov8 Hours have been known to attract as many as 100 people.

'Innovation is a professional stress release', says O'Donnell, 'because it allows you to positively talk about how to solve something, or to talk about how to bring a new idea to life from scratch. There's energy injected into everybody who attends Innov8 Hours, even if they weren't presenting. People attend with a level of positivity. So not only is it a great avenue for giving people a chance to feel acknowledged and respected, but the audience walks away with a great deal of energy and understanding of the importance of innovation.'

As well as recognising innovation internally, O'Donnell says that a few years ago the organisation wanted to start thinking about recognition beyond internal initiatives. O'Donnell felt that a natural evolution was to consider involving the company's biggest suppliers in the innovation journey. So in 2010 the Coca-Cola Amatil Supplier of the Year Awards were launched. The company's top suppliers are invited to pen an entry that describes, among other things, the biggest innovation they have produced that has helped Coca-Cola Amatil. The winners are then announced in a grand award ceremony.

Supplier relationships had previously been thought of as more transactional—they were leveraged to provide excellent goods or services and were primarily evaluated on the basis of being the most cost-effective and highest quality. But by inviting the network of suppliers to participate in innovation, Innov8 flourished. 'Being able to leverage all of their brain power was brilliant', says O'Donnell. 'And all of their technical expertise in their core competencies helped solve issues for our organisation, and indeed our customers, which has been incredibly valuable for Coca-Cola Amatil.'

★★★

Several years ago I had a meeting with the head of innovation at a large Australian government-owned organisation. She began to tell me about the organisation's burgeoning innovation program. She told me about an online suggestion box that had recently been launched and how the focus of the program was to collect as many ideas as possible. I asked her how she was eliciting ideas from employees.

'We pay people $10 per idea', she replied.

'How many ideas do you have so far?' I asked.

'Hundreds. It's been an incredibly popular program so far.'

I then asked her about the quality of the ideas she had received. 'To be honest', she began, 'there are not a lot of great ideas there. People have suggested things such as having free fruit on Fridays, and investing in thicker toilet paper in the staff bathrooms. I haven't seen anything yet that really promises to transform the organisation'.

I wasn't surprised by what she told me, but I was curious as to what she thought about one other thing.

'What do you think would happen if you stopped giving employees $10 for every idea?' I asked.

She considered this for a moment and replied, 'We probably wouldn't get any more ideas'.

The research into the impact of financial rewards on innovation certainly backs up this experience — although the relationship is not completely straightforward. Yu Zhou, from the Renmin University of China, and his colleagues set out to investigate the impact of financial rewards, such as pay rises, performance linked-bonuses, and team-based bonuses, on innovative behaviours. They also examined the impact of non-financial rewards, such as receiving recognition, on innovative behaviours at work. Two hundred and sixteen employees from a variety of Chinese companies were recruited into the study and asked about how they were recognised and rewarded within their organisations, and were also asked to reflect on their own innovative behaviours.

Zhou and his colleagues found that financial rewards did lead to an increase in innovative behaviours — but only up to a point. They found a U-shaped relationship between the variables, in that innovative behaviours increased with some financial rewards, but as the financial rewards increased, innovation actually started to decrease. In contrast, the relationship between non-financial rewards, such as recognition, was a linear one. The greater the non-financial rewards, the greater the innovative behaviours.

Markus Baer, from the University of Illinois Urbana-Champaign, and his colleagues were interested in exploring the impact of financial rewards on employee creativity, and whether this relationship was influenced by the complexity of an employee's job. The researchers recruited 171 people from two American manufacturing companies and asked them about the types of rewards they received for innovation, and about the complexity of their job. Each person's supervisor was then asked to rate their employee's creativity and innovation performance.

Baer found that financial rewards had very different effects on creativity, depending on how complex and challenging a person's job was. For those with more complex jobs, an increase in financial rewards led to a decrease in innovation. However, for those in simple jobs, financial rewards actually increased the person's creative performance.

Indiana University Professor of Entrepreneurship Dean Shepherd and colleague Dawn DeTienne also explored the complex relationship between financial rewards and innovation. Shepherd and DeTienne were interested in examining how having a deep understanding of the customer and their frustrations relates to the effectiveness of financial rewards on innovation. They hypothesised that a deep customer understanding would actually reduce the effectiveness of financial rewards on innovation. In contrast, they felt that those who did not have strong customer knowledge would be more motivated by financial rewards when it came to producing ideas.

The experiment they set up involved people being briefed on problems that customers had experienced with footwear. One group was presented with a large range of issues and frustrations (presented as real quotes from focus groups), while the second group received a more limited set of customer problems. Participants were then instructed to generate ideas for solving these customer problems. In addition, they were told that there was a financial reward for the best solution generated. One group was told the reward was $50, while the other group was told the reward was a measly $1.

The amount of prior knowledge presented to participants had a significant impact on how motivated they were by the financial reward. The size of the reward was a big motivating factor for those with less knowledge about the customer and their problems. The offer of a $50 reward led to these participants generating significantly more ideas than the offer of a $1 reward. In addition, the $50 reward group's ideas were judged to be significantly more innovative than the $1 reward group's ideas.

In stark contrast, financial rewards had almost the opposite effect for participants with a comprehensive knowledge of customer problems. The size of the financial reward had no impact on the number of solutions generated. But, more importantly, the $50 reward group put forward solutions that were evaluated as being less innovative than those from the $1 reward group.

These results may seem surprising. Why would a bigger prize decrease innovation output? The researchers suggest that having a large amount of knowledge (and thus a high level of skill) is a motivator in and of itself, and the financial reward actually gets in the way of this motivation.

★★★

The single biggest problem with financial rewards, however, is that as soon as they are taken away, and assuming that no intrinsic motivators (such as a sense of challenge and autonomy) are in place, motivation for innovation evaporates. After all, if you are only innovating to gain a financial reward, why would you continue to innovate when that reward gets taken away? As such, when given the choice between intrinsic rewards such as recognition, or extrinsic rewards, such as money, intrinsic rewards win every time.

> The most motivating kinds of verbal 'rewards' for complex projects are ones that are not expected.

As well as being mindful of the potential downside of financial rewards, it is also worth noting the results of some recent research into the more informal type of recognition that managers can provide. Dr Rebecca Hewett from the University of Greenwich looked at the impact of managers providing verbal rewards, such as saying 'thank you' to their team. Hewett asked a group of workers to complete a survey at the end of each day for two weeks and asked them about their motivation with respect to a task on which they were currently working.

When it came to simple tasks, verbal rewards from one's manager were very motivating. In contrast, for complex tasks (and innovation projects are invariably complex tasks) standard verbal rewards from a manager failed to motivate. Sometimes these predictable verbal rewards even decreased motivation. The motivation essentially came from being able to get on and make progress. The most motivating kinds of verbal 'rewards' for complex projects are ones that are not expected.

★★★

One final point to consider when it comes to providing recognition is that it's important to be deliberate about what you provide recognition for. It can be tempting to just recognise great innovation performance, but research has shown that recognising the *effort* people have put into innovation is just as (if not more) important. The importance and impact of this need can actually be traced as far back as childhood.

Stanford University psychology professor Carol Dweck has been researching motivation since the 1960s, and is one of the most highly regarded researchers in her field. Not only has she investigated motivation in adults, but she has also conducted research into children and how our mindset development is influenced by the feedback we receive from others. One of the concepts she has explored is the extent to which children believe intelligence is something that is fixed or malleable. Those who believe intelligence is fixed think that you are given a certain amount of intelligence and there is nothing you can do to control or increase it. She referred to these children as having a 'fixed mindset'. Those who believe that intelligence is malleable think that it can be developed through hard work, study and education. Dweck referred to these children as having a 'growth mindset'. She has conducted numerous studies looking at the impact these very different mindsets have on behaviour and performance.

In one study, Lisa Blackwell, Kali Trzesniewski and Dweck studied 373 students who were entering seventh grade at a New York secondary school. At the beginning of the study, all students were surveyed to determine their mindset. Students were asked the extent to which they agreed or disagreed with statements such as 'You have a certain amount of intelligence, and you really can't do much to change it' through to 'You can always greatly change how intelligent you are'. Students were also asked about their learning goals at school, through agreement with statements such as 'An important reason why I do my school work is because I like to learn new things' and 'I like school work that I'll learn from even if I make a lot of mistakes'. Not surprisingly, students with a growth mindset were much more likely to believe that learning was a much more important goal at school than achieving high grades.

The students were also asked about the amount of effort they put into their school work, by indicating their level of agreement with statements such as 'The harder you work at something, the better you will be at it' and 'To tell the truth, when I work hard at my schoolwork, it makes me feel like I'm not very smart'. Students with a fixed mindset were far more likely to view making an effort as a negative behaviour—as though trying hard meant that you had low ability. And when met with a bad grade, those with a fixed mindset were actually more likely to study less – and even consider cheating to improve their grades.

The researchers followed these students for two years, and specifically tracked their performance in maths class. Maths was chosen because it is a subject that typically becomes significantly more challenging as high school progresses.

At the beginning of the study, regardless of mindset, students' scores did not differ significantly on their maths tests. But by as early as the end of first semester, the results achieved by the growth mindset group overtook those with a fixed mindset group. By the end of grade 8, the results obtained by the growth mindset group were significantly higher than the fixed mindset group.

But rather than just leave it at that, the researchers decided to stage an intervention with a subset of the students. They wanted to see if those with a fixed mindset could actually be trained to develop a growth mindset. Students in the experimental group received eight workshops that taught them about the brain and how malleable it is, and that intelligence is something that can be developed with hard work and study. A control group was taught about the brain, but without a focus on its malleability. Teachers (who did not know which students had which mindset) were then asked to monitor students' behaviour and, specifically, their levels of motivation.

The differences were striking—in the control group, only 9 per cent of students were reported to show positive change. However, in the group that had been taught how malleable the brain and intelligence actually was, three times as many students were observed to show positive change in their behaviour. One of the maths teachers commented about a couple of students in the experimental group:

> L., who never puts in any extra effort and doesn't turn in homework on time, actually stayed up late working for hours to finish an assignment early so I could review it and give him a chance to revise it. He earned a B1 on the assignment (he had been getting C's and lower).

> M. was [performing] far below grade level. During the past several weeks, she has voluntarily asked for extra help from me during her lunch period in order to improve her test-taking performance. Her grades drastically improved from failing to an 84 [on] her recent exam.

One of the things parents can do is praise children for effort rather than for talent. Saying to your child, 'Wow, that's a really good score. You must have tried really hard', rather than 'Wow, that's a really good score. You must be smart at this', has been shown to improve persistence and learning, and ultimately create a growth mindset.

These concepts have important implications for the workplace when it comes to innovation. Creating an environment where people are praised for their efforts as opposed to their achievements has been shown to have a significant effect in creating a culture where people feel more comfortable embracing innovation, and also in taking a risk —which is a critical ingredient of innovation. So rather than taking the obvious path of recognising achievements, also take time to recognise effort.

Recognition

# KEY POINTS

- Find opportunities to recognise innovation both formally and informally. This may be in the form of an annual awards night, through to providing regular opportunities for innovators to share their work with others.

- While having an annual awards ceremony for innovation is a fantastic idea, ensure you introduce more regular and frequent opportunities to recognise great innovation.

- Consider giving 'time' (to work on innovation projects) as a reward for innovation efforts.

- As well as recognising people within your organisation, consider how you could recognise great innovation from suppliers, partners and customers.

- Financial rewards will only increase motivation up to a point. In addition, financial rewards are far less effective for those who feel challenged by their role, have a high degree of skill, and have a thorough knowledge of the customer.

- When given the choice between rewarding people through recognition versus money, recognition wins hands-down.

- When giving people verbal rewards, such as a thank-you, the most motivating kind are the unexpected ones.

- Don't just recognise achievements. Make sure you also recognise effort.

# PART II
# **TEAM-LEVEL** FACTORS

In 2009 Dr Ute Hülsheger, an associate professor of work and organisational psychology at Maastricht University, and her colleagues Neil Anderson and Jesus Salgado conducted what has to date been the largest meta-analysis of team-level predictors of innovation. They reviewed the past three decades of research into teams and innovation, specifically looking for studies that had examined the characteristics and behaviour that predict innovation performance in teams.

Their search was extremely thorough. They examined all the studies that had been published on creativity and innovation (across multiple languages), searched through a number of top-tier psychology and management journals and pored over the reference lists in these research papers. After eliminating any papers that were not specifically focused on team-level variables, they ended up with a stack of 91 articles. Within these 91 papers there were 104 independent studies that reported on a total of 50 096 participants.

The results of this meta-analysis, which mirror the results of the larger meta-analysis conducted in 2007 by Samuel Hunter and his colleagues Katrina Bedell and Michael Mumford (see the introduction), are presented over the following three chapters. And if you are currently working in a team that you feel could do with an innovation injection, these chapters contain plenty of food for thought, and practical suggestions you can start to apply immediately.

Chapter 4 looks at the importance of ensuring that all team members feel intellectually stimulated by their peers. Working in an environment where debate and discussion and different points of view are encouraged is key to creating a culture of innovation.

Chapter 5 examines the importance of having a supportive team—a team where people actively listen to and encourage their peers to come up with new ideas, share those ideas and then, as a team, pursue those ideas. This chapter looks at ways to foster this type of environment.

Finally, chapter 6 discusses the importance of collaboration —both within your own team and across other teams within your organisation. This chapter also looks at what happens when collaboration is absent from the team environment, and the negative impact this has on innovation.

# CHAPTER 4

# DEBATE

## Walking in stupid, and other ways to fuel innovation

You may have never heard of Wieden+Kennedy, but I can guarantee that you have seen its work. Wieden+Kennedy is one of the world's top creative advertising agencies. One of the agency's founders, Dan Wieden, was responsible for coming up with one of the most famous taglines on the planet: Nike's 'Just Do It'. In recent years you might have watched actor Isaiah Mustafa riding a white horse backwards, claiming he was 'The man your man could smell like' and thus reviving the Old Spice brand. Or perhaps you remember the agency's 2008 Super Bowl ad for Coca-Cola that featured two huge inflatable cartoon characters chasing a giant inflatable bottle of Coca-Cola across New York City, with an inflatable Charlie Brown emerging victorious having caught the Coke bottle. *Adweek* named it best Super Bowl ad of the decade.

One of the factors that has been identified as critical for creating a culture where innovation thrives is ensuring that different points of view are encouraged and that ideas are regularly debated. And at Wieden+Kennedy, challenging the status quo and debating different views is par for the course.

One of the first things visitors to the London office see is a shop-window mannequin that has a blender for a head. The mannequin is carrying a briefcase that has the words 'Walk in stupid every morning' written on it. The message represents something that cofounder Dan Wieden believes in strongly: that is, that to find innovative ideas, people need to throw away all their assumptions and preconceived ideas.

Neil Christie, who heads up Wieden+Kennedy's London office, says, 'The mannequin is there so it's the first thing you see when you walk in the door, to remind you that that's what we're here to do. If you listen to conventional wisdom or think that the thing you did last time is going to work again this time around, then you're going to lose. You have to assume that conventional wisdom isn't going to work or the category norms aren't going to work.

'It's not that we're encouraging people to be stupid. It's more that we're encouraging people to recognise that they don't necessarily know the answers and that the most experienced people won't necessarily have the answers either. Sometimes you're going to get a fresher answer from somebody looking at it naively, or from a different perspective than the so-called experts.'

One of the ways the tenet 'Walk in stupid every morning' is applied is in the way staff are allocated to clients. In most advertising agencies, people are allocated to clients where they have significant industry experience. For example, if an agency is pitching for a cosmetics account, they typically identify everyone who has worked on beauty brands before, and put them on the team. Clients naturally love this because it makes them feel as if they have 'industry experts' working on their account. But at Wieden+Kennedy this idea gets flipped on its head. People are deliberately assigned to accounts where they don't have oodles of experience in the category.

The Honda account is one example of this strategy in practice. 'There's a reason why most automotive advertising looks the same', explains Christie. And that reason is that people who have experience working on automotive advertising—whether that be as a creative in an advertising agency, a producer, or a director—are generally selected to work on the account because they have years, if not decades, of experience.

So rather than go down this path with Honda, the agency instead put together a team of people who were not automotive veterans. Indeed, some of the people on the team didn't even particularly like cars. But the work the agency produced for Honda was unlike anything else the industry had ever seen.

The Honda Cog commercial is one of the most famous and effective pieces of work that the agency has ever produced. It was released in 2003 and featured a series of Honda Accord automotive parts colliding into each other like dominoes with the ad climaxing with a Honda Accord rolling off the trailer to the line 'Isn't it nice when things just work?' It is one of the most awarded commercials in history.

In a similar vein to Wieden+Kennedy, Laszlo Bock describes in *Work Rules!* how at Google, the least important attribute they look for when recruiting is whether the applicant has had a large amount of experience in the type of role they are applying for.

*Our reasoning and experience is that someone who has done the same task—successfully—for many years is likely to see a situation at Google and replicate the same solution that has worked for them. The problem with this approach is that you lose the opportunity to create something new.*

We apply a similar approach at Inventium. Rather than look for people who have previously worked as innovation consultants, we have instead tried to build a cross-disciplinary team—the commonality being a passion for both science and innovation. We have MBAs, organisational psychologists, entrepreneurs, engineers and economists. We have people who have worked in some of the biggest organisations in the world, and some who have only worked in start-ups. They are all trained in Inventium's intellectual property and contribute to making it better, and when we all get together to solve problems for our clients the results are infinitely better than if we had recruited only people who have had similar jobs in the past.

Debate

Infosys is one of the largest IT consulting firms in the world. It is headquartered in Bangalore, India, and has over 170000 employees spread across the globe. In the early 1990s the leadership team at Infosys realised that despite senior executives being largely middle-aged, the average age of employees was much younger—a spritely 26 years old. What management realised about these younger employees is that, in general, they kept their opinions to themselves—most probably for fear of speaking up or disagreeing with their seniors.

In response, the executive leadership team launched a program called Voice of Youth, with the aim being to elicit the views of this younger generation and to help encourage more debate in leadership team meetings. Top-performing employees in their twenties were hand-picked on the basis of their being high performers, and invited to have a seat on Infosys' management council. But rather than being invited to just attend the meetings, they were actively encouraged to put forward their views, disagree with the views being expressed by the management team, and debate and critique any and all aspects of the organisation. The program proved to be extremely fruitful in opening up all sorts of new views and opinions. It helped shape Infosys's culture into a much stronger one, and enabled the leadership team to stay on top of trends in technology that the younger generation were much more connected to.

★★★

When it comes to encouraging debate, the greater the number of points of view, the more robust the debate will be. And when it comes to innovation and creativity, many research studies have shown the benefit of breadth over depth. People who have a greater breadth of experience and knowledge consistently come up with more creative solutions to problems than those who have perhaps sacrificed breadth for depth in their career and experiences.

Buzz Products, a global product design agency that recruits people with wide-ranging interests and experiences, recently ran a Go Wide program.

'Everyone in the company was given $500', says Managing Director Barry Gold. 'The idea was they had to use the money to learn a new skill or to participate in some sort of activity. Ideally something a little bit challenging and not related to work. People did such cool things, like learning Arabic, doing a DJ course, and skydiving. One story that stood out for me was a girl in the business who was scared of flying and she used her $500 to do a course that helped her get over that. It was great because now she is going on overseas holidays and business trips and it has had an amazing impact on her life and career, as well as it being great that she has overcome a phobia.'

★★★

Having a diverse team can be a great way of sparking debate ... or so, at least, many researchers have thought. However, when Dr Ute Hülsheger and her colleagues began to examine the findings around team diversity and innovation performance, they found conflicting results. Some research indicated that diversity was a good thing (as one would intuitively expect). However, other studies reported it to negatively affect innovation.

> A team that demonstrates good job-relevant diversity is typically cross-functional, and has a good spread of educational backgrounds and expertise.

After looking more deeply into these research studies, Hülsheger began to pull apart the two main types of diversity that the research had been examining. Some studies had examined job-relevant diversity, such as the types of skills and experience people bring to their roles. A team that demonstrates good job-relevant diversity is typically cross-functional, and has a good spread of different educational backgrounds and expertise.

Other studies examined the effect of background diversity (factors such as age, gender and ethnicity — that is, nothing relevant to people's actual job). Hülsheger and her team found that the data suggested that background diversity actually has a negative impact on innovation. Explanations of this negative correlation postulated that background diversity causes communication problems and also that this kind of diversity might lead to problems in reaching consensus — which of course, would halt innovation efforts.

In contrast, the researchers found that job-relevant diversity is significantly related to innovation performance. Having people from different functional backgrounds, people who have studied different skills at university, and people who have learned different skills during their career, is a very positive team dimension for innovation.

What researchers do not know is whether the relationship between job-relevant diversity and innovation is a linear one. It is possible that the relationship is curvilinear, in that there might be a point at which too much diversity actually starts to decrease innovation. In addition, the positive effect of job-relevant diversity may be stronger in teams that have worked together for a long time than in those who are newly formed and are yet to develop their own norms.

What this means for your organisation, especially if staff turnover is low, is that rather than letting birds of a feather flock together, you should focus instead on curating teams to ensure job-relevant skills and experience are diverse. This should be considered especially important in teams that are coming together to solve tough innovation challenges.

Dae Mellencamp, president of Vimeo, describes how all project teams within her organisation are pulled from different parts of the business. 'On any given project, we will almost always have small cross-functional teams. We would typically bring together someone from Product, someone from the Community area and a Content person to work together to come up with ideas, and then to work on it together to solve all the detailed issues. What we've been finding is that this leads to really, really great work.'

★★★

Signalling that debate is encouraged is something that should start in the recruitment process. Most recruitment processes consist of barely more than a couple of interviews conducted by someone from HR or a recruitment company, and then a line manager. Ironically, these processes are structured to find clones of ourselves, to discourage diversity, and to find people who have an immaculate knowledge of the job they are about to do.

We know from research that we are far more likely to hire people who remind us of ourselves. Lauren Rivera, an assistant professor at Northwestern University's Kellogg School of Management, conducted research into 120 hiring managers and the factors influencing their hiring decisions. She found that rather than hiring the most qualified applicants for the job, hiring managers were significantly more likely to recruit people they thought they could be friends with—people like them.

Rivera describes the story of a hiring manager at a law firm who was looking through a job applicant's CV and saw his resume listed hobbies such as lacrosse and squash. The hiring manager decided to reject this applicant because the culture of the firm was more 'rough and tumble'. Another candidate was rejected for being too intellectual (he had expressed an interest in eighteenth-century literature).

Another common issue with typical recruitment processes is that applicants tend to meet only their manager and, if they are lucky, perhaps a couple of peers. Rarely do applicants meet people who would be reporting directly to them. Google flips this common process on its head: all potential managers will meet at least one or two of the people who will be reporting to them. 'We find that the best candidates leave subordinates feeling inspired and excited to learn from them,' explains Laszlo Bock, senior vice president of people operations at Google, in his book *Work Rules!*

Having applicants meet a couple of their direct reports sends a signal that the organisation is non-hierarchical—that it gives power directly to subordinates, who generally have little power. And any signal that can be sent about an organisation being non-hierarchical will do wonders for encouraging great debate and discussion when subordinates don't see eye-to-eye with their superiors.

★★★

In a similar vein to Google's take on the recruitment process, Jack Welch flipped the idea of traditional mentoring on its head when he was CEO of General Electric. The idea for 'reverse mentoring' came about when Welch was in London in the 1990s, speaking to a fellow CEO who was describing a project he was on in which he was a mentee. Welch responded in shock, asking why he—someone

Debate

heading up an organisation—was a mentee. It turned out that it was an e-business project about which this CEO knew very little. So in order to get up to speed, he found what he described as the smartest person under 30 in his organisation and brought them in as a mentor.

Welch loved this idea so much so that within 48 hours he 'tipped the organisation upside down'. The brightest young sparks at GE were paired up with Welch's top 500 executives. Welch himself had a mentor who was in his twenties and taught him how to surf the internet. A decade later, Twitter and Facebook were common topics for the reverse mentor relationships.

While many organisations, such as Hewlett-Packard and Cisco, have set up informal reverse-mentoring relationships, if you are serious about bringing this concept to your organisation, here are a few things to consider:

1  *Be clear on the business objectives you want the program to achieve.* In the case of innovation, it might be about encouraging debate between employees, breaking down silos (so mentors are paired with mentees who work in a completely different area of the business) and exposing employees to broader knowledge than they would otherwise be exposed to.

2  *Set metrics to allow you to measure success.* The easiest way to do this is to design survey items that measure the variables you are trying to affect. Get a pre-program baseline from all participants, and survey people again at the end of the program. You might even choose to take a third measurement three months after the program to identify which changes outlasted the program.

3  *Ask for mentee volunteers.* It is generally more challenging to get senior leaders to volunteer to be mentees, as more-junior people are generally queueing up to be involved and form a relationship with someone senior. If you are having trouble getting interest, consider appointing an executive sponsor who may ask certain leaders to be involved and can effectively convince them of the benefits. Once you have a group of leaders who are willing to be involved, you can then put the call out to mentors.

4   *Pair up the mentees with mentors.* Ideally, you want to pair
    up people who work in completely separate parts of the
    organisation, which will help in breaking down silos.
    Functional diversity is also beneficial. For example, you
    don't want two people with marketing backgrounds coming
    together; you want the relationship to be about exposing the
    mentee to completely new knowledge that they wouldn't
    have otherwise been exposed to. And don't let geographic
    boundaries get the way — technology such as Skype and
    Google Hangouts make it easy for remote mentoring sessions
    to occur.

5   *Give some suggestions for the structure of the mentoring relationship.*
    For example, how regularly people should meet, and how
    long meetings should go for. You might want to provide
    some topics for conversation, such as emerging technologies
    that the mentor is in touch with, and perhaps even ask the
    mentee to come prepared with questions they want answered.
    You should also think about how long the mentoring
    relationship should go for — presumably, it will have an end
    point.

6   *Revisit your metrics and evaluate the program.* I have found
    most well-run reverse mentoring programs to be extremely
    successful, so if the metrics are pointing in the right direction,
    hopefully it can become a regular part of your organisation's
    innovation program.

One final point to consider is that while debate is something that
should be encouraged at a team level, it is always important for
senior leaders within the organisation to walk the talk. If senior
leaders are not open to being challenged and engaging in debate,
it becomes very difficult for this kind of openness to filter down
to the team level. Dae Mellencamp, president of Vimeo, is a great
example of a leader who truly encourages debate. 'People know
that I'm movable', she explains. 'I don't come in being black or
white. I watch first before I decide. You can convince me if you
have the right arguments.

Debate

'It's sincere on my part because I don't think I know everything. That ability to challenge and debate is so critical because you can't innovate unless people feel they can do this. Teams at Vimeo feel very strongly that they can fight for what they believe in. I think that's critical because if you lose that and you squish that, you squish the creativity. You squish the innovation.'

# KEY POINTS

- Consider how the phrase 'Walk in stupid every morning' could help you and your team get better at challenging the status quo, refrain from making assumptions, and ultimately encourage a wider range of views when working on innovation projects.

- Avoid the temptation to recruit people who are just like you—doing so will only discourage debate and encourage homogeneity of thinking.

- Having a greater breadth (rather than depth) of knowledge and experience has been shown to be beneficial for creativity. Consider ways in which you and your team can enhance your own breadth.

- Job-related diversity has been found to be important in driving innovation, so when curating teams, try to find a good mix of functional backgrounds. In contrast, demographic diversity has shown to actually decrease innovation efforts.

- Consider implementing a reverse mentoring program to help break down silos, help senior people gain a greater breadth of knowledge, and encourage debate and discussion in relationships between people in your organisation who previously did not know each other.

- Ensure that senior leaders remain open to being challenged and engaging in debate—that is, that they lead by example.

# CHAPTER 5
# TEAM SUPPORTIVENESS

'What did you say you were called?' and other factors that influence teamwork

I recently worked with a leadership team within a national retailer. I was brought in to run a multiday workshop to help them, among other things, refine their innovation strategy. It was one of the most challenging three days I have had at Inventium. I'm fairly lucky at Inventium, as the vast majority of our clients are really smart, passionate people. They care deeply about innovation and making a positive difference to their organisation and the industry they play in. But this team was different.

First, they didn't listen to each other. About nine or ten times per day, the team would be arguing about something and then someone would speak up and say 'You are both saying the same thing'. That is, they were both arguing exactly the same point, but because they failed to listen to each other, they hadn't realised it. Rather than listen to each other, it was as if people were simply waiting in line to talk.

Second, almost every single strategy or idea suggested was shot down. Ideas were met with retorts such as 'We tried that last year and it didn't work' or 'That will never get the support of the wider business' or 'We won't be able to get the resources to execute that'. And when certain strategies and ideas *did* get up, individuals who did not support them simply zoned out because they hadn't got their own way.

Third, there was no trust between the group members. Relationships ranged from passive-aggressive through to overtly aggressive. People argued with each other, and even seemed to appear energised by the arguing.

> Having teams that are open, trusting and supportive of each other is a critical driver of an innovation culture.

Having teams that are open, trusting and supportive of each other is a critical driver of an innovation culture. And so, needless to say, the culture within this team, and more broadly within the division, was one that did not breed innovation.

Let's go back to the 1940s for a moment, to one of the pioneers of child psychology, psychiatrist John Bowlby. It was through clinical observations and research studies into childhood emotions and behaviour that Bowlby developed one of the most prevalent theories of childhood development: attachment theory. The basic premise of attachment theory is that children need to feel a secure connection to at least one primary caregiver (usually the mother or father—or both) in order to feel comfortable and confident in exploring the outside world. Without this sense of attachment and security, children become fearful of exploration and trying out new experiences.

By chance, an American developmental psychologist, Mary Ainsworth, had accompanied her husband to London, where he was to complete his doctoral studies. While in London, Ainsworth happened to see a job advertisement for a researcher in Bowlby's team—specifically focusing on the effects of being separated from one's mother on a child's personality development.

Ainsworth led the first empirical study into attachment theory, following on from Bowlby's work. The research took place in Uganda, where Ainsworth observed 26 families with children aged between one and 24 months. She visited these families once a fortnight for nine months. After analysing the data from these regular visits, she confirmed Bowlby's theories that infants who were more securely attached to their mother cried less and were much more confident in exploring their surrounding environment.

So what, you may ask, does the behaviour of infants have to do with promoting a culture of innovation? Quite a lot, actually.

★★★

Ute Hülsheger and her colleagues found that cohesion is one of the biggest determinants of team performance in innovation. Cohesive teams are ones in which people are not frightened of being mocked if they come up with a crazy idea, but instead feel secure enough within their team to challenge the status quo and put forward all sorts of suggestions and ideas. Like infants feeling confident enough to explore if they feel securely attached to their parent, so too will employees feel free to explore new ideas if they feel comfortable and safe with their team.

In a study focused on team support, communication and cohesiveness and how that affects the success of innovation projects, Professor Martin Hoegl from Washington State University investigated the behaviour of 145 software development teams in Germany. Hoegl and his colleague Hans Georg Gemuenden used a six-factor framework for looking at the quality of interaction and support that occurs within a team.

1 *Communication*—the frequency, openness and informality of the exchange of information between team members.

2 *Coordination*—a common understanding of the current status of projects and individuals' contributions to them.

3 *Mutual support*—individuals within the team being cooperative rather than competitive with each other.

Team supportiveness

4   *Balance of member contributions*—team members being able to contribute all relevant knowledge and experience to the team.

5   *Effort*—individuals contributing an equally high level of effort to tasks.

6   *Cohesion*—team members having a strong team spirit and being motivated to remain on the team.

After measuring the software development teams on the six factors, Hoegl also investigated the success of innovation projects that the teams had implemented. Success was defined first in terms of the quality of the innovation and the efficiency of the process of creating it (rated by managers, team leaders and the team members), and second, by the team members' satisfaction with the experience of working on the innovation project.

Hoegl found that the six factors of team interaction and support significantly predicted the outcomes of innovation projects—both in terms of the quality of the innovation and the efficiency in creating it. In addition, team interaction, not surprisingly, predicted the amount of satisfaction the teams said they had experienced while creating the innovation.

Professor Michael West and Michaela Wallace, from the University of Sheffield, were interested in studying how effectively communication and support occurred within a team, and its impact on innovation culture and outputs. They selected several teams within the UK healthcare industry, consisting of doctors and nurses. Three of the teams they studied were classed as non-innovative or 'traditional' teams and five of the teams were classed as highly innovative (based on independent evaluations).

The researchers asked the teams about how the members worked together, with respect to supporting each other with problem-solving, communicating with each other openly and honestly, and valuing each other's experience (rather than status or job title). At the same time, six independent judges rated the innovations that each team had implemented over the last two years.

When West analysed the data he found that team supportiveness and cohesion had a very significant impact on the innovativeness of projects that had been implemented by each team. It in fact accounted for 29 per cent of the variance. Essentially, this means that nearly a third of the innovativeness of projects could be ascribed to how supportive and cohesive teams were.

Research by Professor Teresa Amabile and Dr Stanley Gryszkiewicz investigated the impact of team dynamics on creative performance in R&D labs. The researchers interviewed 120 R&D scientists and asked them to describe two events: one exemplifying a project that led to a highly creative outcome, and one that exemplified a project that did not lead to creative outcomes. The scientists were then asked to describe the central characters in their two narratives, specifically focusing on the characteristics of the people and environment involved.

Amabile and Gryszkiewicz found collaborative and cooperative team behaviour was critical to producing creative outcomes. Extending this environment to other divisions within the organisation was also very significant. One scientist remarked, 'Having other scientists to talk to is important. When it came time to introduce the product, I had support from different areas... which enabled its coming to the marketplace'. The researchers also found, not surprisingly, that a lack of collaboration was detrimental to creativity.

★★★

In terms of structuring a team for innovation success, it is vitally important to ensure that there is what researchers term 'goal interdependence'. Hülsheger defines this as 'the extent to which team members' goals and rewards are related in such a way that an individual team member can only reach his or her goal if the other team members achieve their goals as well'. So rather than a bunch of independent individual goals, having team goals has a much bigger impact on a team's innovation performance.

There are a few different ways that teams can achieve goal interdependence. First, rather than providing solely individual feedback to members of the team, this can be mixed up with feedback to the team as a whole. When people receive team-level feedback, it is made clear that each individual's behaviour affects the team, and thus team performance.

Team supportiveness

Second, performance evaluations and rewards should be linked to the goals of the team. By doing this, the team will be motivated to work together effectively so that evaluations are seen as positive steps towards achieving team goals and rewards.

What is interesting to note is that *task* interdependence (where team members are reliant on each other to complete certain tasks) is not significantly related to innovation performance. So while it is important to ensure that the team is working towards a goal that is reliant on the contribution of each member, each team member's tasks will be different, depending on their role in contributing to the overall team goal.

★★★

As well as team goals, teams also need a clear vision. 'Vision' is usually thought of as something only managers need be concerned with as an organisation-wide driver of innovation and performance. However, Hülsheger and her colleagues found that teams that had a clear, guiding and motivating vision performed significantly more innovatively than teams who did not have this in place.

> ...rather than a bunch of independent individual goals, having team goals has a much bigger impact on a team's innovation performance.

A vision is not just about having clear, overriding objectives; it is also about the team committing to achieving these objectives — in other words, buying into the vision. Having a strong vision and committing to this allows teams to have a shared sense of purpose and responsibility towards each other.

At construction company Mirvac, Group General Manager of Innovation Christine Gilroy, has given a lot of thought to curating teams that will be supportive and play to each other's strengths. Gilroy was tasked with putting together teams of people who would work on some of the company's biggest innovation challenges — their innovation missions.

'We have eight innovation missions that are aligned to our innovation strategy', says Gilroy. 'We put together completely diverse teams that work on those missions. The mission might be a retail mission, but we'll have someone from finance working on that team, or it might be a residential property mission and we'll have people from administration working on that team. They bring that fresh perspective and they don't bring assumptions to that problem. It's so beneficial, and I've seen it work in practice over and over again. The teams are progressing much faster than if it were just a team of experts or just a team of people who knew nothing about the problem.'

When the teams first started working on the innovation missions, one member from each team was given the title of team leader. But during the first few weeks of the teams working on their projects, it occurred to Gilroy that one of the things that was important to the innovation program was to try to have a flat hierarchy where everyone was at the same level.

Gilroy began to notice that something as simple as a title had the power to completely change the dynamic of the teams. The team leader took charge, and often all responsibility ultimately fell into their hands. To keep things flat and to keep workload even, Gilroy decided to 'demote' the team leaders to team administrators. Their role changed to looking after the logistics of the team and ensuring they were meeting regularly and communicating effectively.

'The change in title sent the message that everyone in the team is equal, and their voice is equal', explains Gilroy. 'I constantly reinforce to the teams that even if they don't work in retail, if they are working on a retail mission, then their opinion and voice is just as, if maybe

*(continued)*

Team supportiveness

not more, important than someone who already works in that area. I want to make sure that we are creating that environment where people feel they can have an opinion even if they aren't experts in that field, because otherwise it can be quite intimidating.'

Changing the team leader title led to an enormous difference in behaviour. 'The leaders were saying, "It's not just me in charge. What do you all think?" It really did lead to that. It was interesting to see how powerful that was to flatten the structure.

'Ultimately, I think the people in the teams felt more empowered. It is easy to sit back and defer to a leader to look for their direction. But without a leader, everyone has a voice and is empowered to express it.'

# KEY POINTS

- Creating an environment where team members feel supported in their thoughts and ideas is critical for creating a culture where people can innovate effectively.

- Six important ingredients to improving the quality of interaction of a team are: communication, coordination, mutual support, balance of member contributions, effort (all members contributing an equally high level of effort to tasks) and cohesion. Reflect on how present these are in your team, and what you can do to improve.

- Consider setting team goals and a team vision to unite team members in a common purpose.

- Err on the side of not using titles that inflate a team member's status, as this will have an impact on how effectively the team works.

# CHAPTER 6

# COLLABORATION

## How to get people working with the un-usual suspects

Most large organisations produce a handbook for employees. The handbook generally talks about the company values, policies and procedures, how to apply for annual leave, and so on. It's the sort of thing you are given on your first day and probably never look at again. Every employee handbook I have ever laid my eyes on would double as a good cure for insomnia. So I reacted with great surprise when a friend of mine said to me a few years ago, 'You should check out Valve's employee handbook—it is awesome!'

I had never heard of Valve—probably because I am not a gamer. But if you *are* a gamer, you probably know exactly who I am talking about. Valve was started in 1996 by two ex-Microsoft employees, Gabe Newell and Mike Harrington. It is the company behind the Half Life series, which by its tenth birthday had sold over 20 million units and picked up over 50 Game of the Year awards. Valve's video game digital distribution system, Steam, had over 75 million active users in 2013, and the company has an estimated value of around US$3 billion.

When starting Valve, Newell and Harrington recognised that finding incredibly talented people and convincing them to come to Valve (and indeed *stay* at Valve) was going to be critical to the company's success. And they felt that the best way to achieve this was to do away with hierarchy, functional departments and managers. *Valve: Handbook for New Employees* explains:

> *Welcome to Flatland. Hierarchy is great for maintaining predictability and repeatability... But when you're an entertainment company that's ... going out of its way to recruit the most intelligent, innovative, talented people on Earth, telling them to sit at a desk and do what they're told obliterates 99 percent of their value.*

As such, when you start at Valve, you don't have a job title and you don't have a manager telling you what to do. Instead you are given a desk — with wheels on it. The wheels are a critical part, as the first big decision employees need to make when they start at Valve is which project team (or cabal) to join. And once you have found one, you simply wheel your desk on over. There is literally nothing in the way to interfere with collaboration between any employee within Valve.

There are no rulebooks when it comes to deciding which project/s you want to work on and who you want to collaborate with. Instead, employees are encouraged to speak to as many people as they can about what projects they are working on. They are then encouraged to ask themselves questions such as 'Of all the projects currently under way, what's the most valuable thing I can be working on?', 'Which project will have the highest direct impact on our customers? How much will the work I ship benefit them?' and 'What's interesting? What's rewarding? What leverages my individual strengths the most?' And, as the handbook says, 'The chair next to anyone's desk is always open, so plant yourself in it often'.

... we know from research that cross-functional and cross-departmental collaboration is a critical driver of an innovation culture.

The way in which the 300-plus employees at Valve operate is vastly different from life at most organisations. On most people's first day at a company they know exactly what team they are on, who their manager is, and where they are supposed to sit. By setting up these structures, employees are essentially taught from day one to stick within their box. But we know from research that cross-functional and cross-departmental collaboration is a critical driver of an innovation culture.

★★★

One of the ways global pharmaceutical company Pfizer encourages cross-departmental collaboration is through Dare to Try champions, part of the organisation-wide innovation program Dare to Try. Within Pfizer, there are 500 champions whose role is to help facilitate innovation across all of the business.

Vice President of Worldwide Innovation Wendy Mayer explains, 'From a collaboration standpoint, the way we've set it up is that we prefer to have the champions work on challenges that are not part of their own business unit. We do that so they're not so close to the challenge that they may be biased, but also it enables people to get a better appreciation of the different challenges that are happening across the organisation and be able to contribute their own unique perspective. Given they work in a different corner of Pfizer, they tend to bring in a different viewpoint, and specifically, they may have a different understanding or different idea of how to address the challenge.'

As part of the Dare to Try program, Mayer and her colleagues are aware that in order to drive innovation, you have to bring together people who come at it from different angles and bring different perspectives. 'The fact that we can bring people together who come from very different parts of the organisation who are all trying to achieve a similar goal really helps expand the creativity and the breadth of ideas. People will work to challenge one another. We've worked as a program team to help facilitate many of those collaborations.'

Mayer explains that in some of Pfizer's smaller markets, particularly in Europe, a lot of the business units have banded together and run sessions that have been about the market as a whole, or about a particular issue that they're addressing that will benefit from input from different areas of the business. 'For example, here in the United States, we have a corporate affairs program where the team has worked on an initiative that is called

Get Old. They've worked on developing opportunities across different business units and ways to express what that program means and how to connect to different parts of our business. Collaboration really helps underscore the ability to bring in different perspectives.'

While Mayer says that people at Pfizer really enjoy collaborating—'It's fun to work with people that you don't get to work with all the time and it's interesting to hear their ideas'—it's not without its challenges. 'It's hard because we're a very big organisation that has lots of different divisions and we are spread all over the world.'

If you suffer from dry lips you have probably, at some point in your life, purchased a ChapStick. ChapStick is a brand that's synonymous with chapped lips. In fact, the ChapStick brand has been so successful that it has a generic trademark. (This happens when a brand name has become synonymous with the product or service category it sits within.) However, in 2013 Eos lip balm overtook the seemingly unbeatable ChapStick to become America's best-selling lip balm.

Eos lip balm was created not by a large cosmetics company, but by an advertising agency called Anomaly—although referring to it as an advertising agency feels like a significant misrepresentation.

Anomaly certainly lives up to its name, and its achievements extend way beyond the lip balm space. You might have seen the agency's 2013 Budweiser Super Bowl commercial, about a Clydesdale coming-of-age story. This ad was the third most-shared Super Bowl spot in history. Or perhaps you have watched Anomaly's collaboration with chef Eric Ripert in the Emmy-winning show *Avec Eric*.

Anomaly's business model is very different from other agencies. Partner Stuart Smith describes it like this: 'We are incentivised differently. We never charge for time. It incentivises the wrong things (i.e. to take longer and put more people on the project). Instead, we have a value-based compensation model, and aim to have a significant component of this compensation be aligned to the commercial success of our clients. Skin in the game, basically. It breeds a different kind of innovative thinking. Real-world innovative thinking. Innovation with consequence. It means our thinking is not just about creativity for the sake of creativity, but for the commercial sake of creativity.'

Collaboration is one of the key parts of Anomaly's model and it's why it is able to create projects as diverse as lip balm, award-winning TV advertisements and Emmy–award winning shows. 'The most important thing we do is to bring in the right kind of team members', explains Smith. 'Our model fundamentally requires collaboration. It can only work if we have people open to, and supportive of, new ideas. All agencies talk about this, but our model necessitates it. Our model is to surround the business challenge with a mix of highly talented people, with different backgrounds and skills, and open minds. Because we surround the business challenge, the answer can be whatever will work best, so we can't have people who assume the answer is to make ads. To achieve that, our team members need to have high talent and low ego, people who will happily give up their own idea if someone else has a better one. If you have people who believe in that, and naturally work like that, then you're more than halfway there.'

At the same time as having breadth through cross-department group diversity, when you have people collaborating on a project you need at least one or two content experts with deep knowledge of the subject matter. Through an analysis of patents that had introduced completely new knowledge or ideas into a field, Professor Sarah Kaplan from the University of Toronto's Rotman School of Management found that these groundbreaking patents needed a very deep level of subject-matter expertise in order to emerge.

★★★

While companies such as Valve, Pfizer and Anomaly make collaboration look easy, making it happen in reality is often one of the biggest challenges organisations face when it comes to creating a culture for innovation. I can't remember a single client of Inventium's ever saying to us, upon our initial meeting, 'People don't operate in silos — we all work together incredibly collaboratively'. In pretty much every introductory meeting I have with new clients, the problem of working in silos (that is, isolated business units or departments that never speak to each other) inevitably gets raised.

We know from the research that working in silos is a creativity killer. Elizabeth Briody, business anthropologist and founder of the consultancy Cultural Keys LLC, and her colleague Ken Erickson, an applied anthropologist from the University of South Carolina, set out to explore the impact of organisational silos on innovation. Data from three major US-based organisations were analysed for the study — an intimate apparel company, a global automotive company (General Motors), and a hospital. Approximately 250 employees were interviewed for the research, and several meetings, general work practices and interactions were observed. The three companies were highly siloed, very hierarchical, and presented employees with little opportunity to move across silos for new career opportunities.

Within the intimate apparel company, the siloed structure had a critical impact on innovation and collaboration. In an interview, one newly hired manager observed, 'We don't meet with panties, and we don't meet with other bras. They are on my floor, but we are not talking among ourselves. We don't feel we are competing, but we don't talk about what worked well...It is kind of a silo here'.

The fact that bras didn't talk to panties had major implications for innovation and also for sales. At one stage, retailers were unable to order enough matching bra and panty sets and so had to stop advertising them to their customers—leading to significant frustrations from both customers and retailers.

The sharing of ideas between sales staff (who were getting direct feedback from customers) and designers was, not surprisingly, very limited. This led to designers just producing what they thought was best, which meant that the customer was essentially left out of the innovation process.

At GM, the researchers studied collaboration between three different business units that had to work together to deliver a specific innovation project. Each business unit had very different decision-making styles (which was particularly apparent in meetings)—ranging from consensus decision-making (in which everyone in the team had to agree before moving forward) through to leader-dictated decision-making (in which the team leader was responsible for all decisions).

These different decision-making styles made the collaboration process extremely difficult, and some important product decisions were made by force and without consensus. The negative consequences of this included management credibility being called into question, delays in decision-making in the product development process, and issues needing to be revisited over and over before being resolved. This resulted in the program being delayed by six months and significant increases in the program's cost.

Ultimately, the problems with the business unit collaboration led to the program being terminated two years after its inception. The program was intended to engender innovation, but was estimated to have cost GM $2.2 million in lost vehicle sales, jeopardised the viability of its global vehicle programs, and called into question its effectiveness as a global manufacturer.

Things were significantly better at the third organisation studied. Patient wait times in the ER were eight hours on average, but could be up to 20 hours, depending on whether the hospital was at full capacity. To help reduce wait time, the hospital put in place a program that required significant collaboration between several different units.

The program required a couple of different units to collaborate effectively with the ER: the diagnostic unit, which was asked to assist by turning around tests quickly; and nurses, who were able to facilitate discharges from the hospital.

Leadership communication proved to be one of the factors critical to collaboration's success, as was the genuine desire of staff to improve the current situation. One of the ER managers from the study described his approach:

> *I met with every manager before starting this study and said, 'Here's our plans. This is where we need to go.' And all of them were receptive—the pharmacy, radiology, the lab. I said, 'We're going to land extra taxing stuff on you. We're going to expect you to turn over these orders relatively quickly. This is going to add a huge workload burden on you. Is this something you're willing to do?' None of them blinked an eye at it. They all said, 'Let's go for it'…They've all jumped in and tackled the issue. It's been a group effort.*

★★★

As Briody's study illustrates, one of the pillars of collaboration is strong communication across the different teams and departments involved in a project. But just as critical to innovation is that team members maintain good relationships and communication with a variety of people outside the team. Through relationships with those outside their immediate team, people gain access to a greater diversity of thoughts, ideas and new perspectives on the problems they are working on. Research has suggested these relationships do not necessarily need to be strong—but that communication with a variety of people outside of the team does need to be relatively frequent.

Giles Hirst, an associate professor of management at Monash University, took this a step further by examining just how important indirect connections can be—that is, connections that are two or more degrees removed from the individual.

Hirst and his colleagues recruited 223 sales representatives at a Chinese pharmaceutical company, and looked at the diversity of information and insights people had access to through their networks. To measure this, they identified how many 'nonredundant' people participants each had in their network. Nonredundant connections were defined as the people with whom the individual does not interact with directly, but rather those people with whom their direct networks interact with.

After measuring the number of nonredundant people in each individual's network, the researchers measured the participants on innovation behaviours, such as how effectively they developed new ways to promote products, their development of ideas to increase client sales, and their identification of ways to connect with sales targets that were tricky to access. The researchers found that there was a strong relationship between employee innovativeness and the number of nonredundant ties within their network.

★★★

Back inside the organisation, there are two ways to think about collaboration—vertically and horizontally.

- *Vertical collaboration* refers to employees feeling comfortable in sharing ideas with their manager and, in turn, their manager having confidence in their suggestions.

Collaboration

- *Lateral collaboration* refers to employees being interested in each other's work, keeping each other informed of work, and being able to share information and knowledge with other employees.

Professor Jozée Lapierre, from Polytechnique Montréal, was interested in the impact on innovation from these two types of collaboration across an organisation.

Lapierre and her colleague Vincent-Pierre Giroux surveyed 122 employees of high-tech firms in Canada. Employees were asked about how they did (or did not) collaborate with others — both above and beside them. The creative output of the organisation was also measured.

The researchers found that vertical and lateral collaboration both had a significant impact on a firm's level of innovation. As such, leaders should ensure that collaboration is driven within and across teams. But ensuring that people feel as if they can collaborate with and get support from their manager is also important (this is discussed in chapter 7).

Verena Mueller, from Justus Liebig University, found that a collectivist and collaborative environment is particularly important when it comes to producing successful breakthrough innovations. Breakthrough, exploratory innovations have a high degree of newness and complexity. As such, organisations that promote good teamwork and collaboration have been shown to be far more effective at fostering these types of innovations.

★★★

One of the things that can make collaboration challenging is that many companies now have flexible work policies, meaning that employees regularly work from outside of the office and, in addition, don't necessarily work standard hours. Given that we like to practice what we preach at Inventium, we gave a lot of thought as to how we could have the best of both worlds.

Our office is quite noisy. The team is packed onto two very large communal tables and people regularly shout across the office to one another when having conversations. There are also several casual meeting areas, and a couple of formal areas too—but with a fast-growing team, quiet space is scarce in our office. As such, we felt it important to have a policy around flexible working hours and places—but with a difference.

Our biggest fear about flexible working arrangements was that if everyone was working their own hours and working away from the office more frequently, we would never all be in the same room. As such, we set Mondays and Fridays as our collaboration days. These are the days when flexible working does not apply. Unless the team has client meetings or workshops, everyone is in the office between 8.30 am and 5 pm. We schedule all team meetings on one of these days, and most of our informal collaboration happens on these days too. Then, from Tuesday to Thursday, the team disperses and people are either out of the office travelling nationally or internationally to help different clients, or are working from home or a café or a library if they want some quiet time to get a solid chunk of solo work done.

The model has worked really well in providing a structure that supports the different working styles and project needs of individuals, but also makes sure that collaboration doesn't fall by the wayside. Fridays, in particular, are filled with team meetings about various projects. If you were to ask the team, Friday tends to be people's favourite day of the week due to the exciting opportunities that get sparked through collaboration.

Collaboration

# KEY POINTS

- Organisational silos have a detrimental impact on innovation. Think about ways you can start to break down these silos.

- Set up a group of innovation champions whose job it is to work across the organisation and encourage collaboration with teams and departments that would never normally work together to solve problems.

- Consider building teams around project briefs like Anomaly does, rather than giving briefs to existing teams.

- If you are feeling particularly brave, consider taking a leaf from Valve and letting newcomers naturally collaborate with any team they desire when deciding which projects to work on.

- If implementing a flexible working policy, consider how it will affect collaboration; potentially have a day or two that is non-flexible to ensure flexible working doesn't make collaboration even more challenging.

# PART III
# LEADER-LEVEL
## FACTORS

A few years ago Inventium was engaged by a global accounting firm to run some innovation capability-building programs. The vast majority of partners were very conservative — from what they wore to work through to their views and attitudes. However, there was one partner who was different from the rest. His 'uniform' was jeans and a t-shirt, he had very liberal views, encouraged people to 'seek forgiveness rather than permission' (that is, just go out and try something rather than waiting to get approval) and was seen as a bit of a maverick by his peers. His style was strongly reflected in his team. Out of all the teams in the firm that we got to know, his was by far the most innovative. They felt free to experiment and try new things out and, by doing so, produced some of the most groundbreaking innovations the firm had ever seen.

Leaders play a critical role in driving innovation. People are hard-wired to take their cues from those 'above' them — a behaviour that starts when we are children and continues through to how we behave at work. The Chinese proverb 'the fish rots from the head down' describes the notion that all problems in an organisation can be traced back to the top. Leaders (particularly the most senior leaders) in an organisation set the tone for how we should behave at work.

This section of the book describes ways in which leaders can deliberately create a culture of innovation. The first chapter in this section examines what supervisors can do to boost innovation performance in the people they directly manage. Research has shown that the behaviour of a supervisor has a very big impact on people's levels of innovation — and inconsistent levels of support at the supervisor level can be one of the biggest inhibitors of innovation in organisations.

Chapter 8 looks at how the very top leaders of an organisation can drive a culture of innovation. While supervisors have a big influence on innovation culture, the impact that senior leaders have is, perhaps not surprisingly, even bigger. Senior leaders need to be perceived as supportive of innovation efforts — if they are not, it is tough to create a consistent, across-the-board culture of innovation.

The way innovation is resourced, in terms of time, money and people, plays a critical role in innovation culture. If people feel that innovation is not being resourced by leaders, this causes cynicism and the perception that leaders are just paying lip-service to innovation. Chapter 9 focuses on how leaders should approach resourcing innovation—from a time, people and money perspective.

Finally, leaders need to set clear goals in order to make innovation thrive. If people are not clear as to what they should be working towards or aiming for, then innovation tends to be curtailed. Chapter 10 covers the types of goals leaders need to be setting, and also what happens when clear goals are not set.

# CHAPTER 7

# SUPERVISOR SUPPORT

## When 'nice' isn't enough

We have all worked for a manager who, when presented with a great idea, instinctively reacts with a comment like 'We tried that three years ago' or 'That will never work'. But what we know is that in innovation cultures senior leaders have the opposite reaction to great ideas (and even not-so-great ones).

Dae Mellencamp, president of Vimeo, describes how she reacts to new ideas. 'One of the things I think I'm good at is I'm a cheerleader. Not literally—I wasn't one in high school—but I get excited about ideas. I'm a complete nerd. I love a great idea and I don't care where it comes from. My standard reaction to a great idea is 'God, that's so awesome. Let's do that!' I know that I don't always have the best idea. I have a good one occasionally. I get excited about my own ideas too. But I get really excited about other people's great ideas.'

If only all managers were like Mellencamp.

★★★

Megan Kachur is responsible for creating new merchandise ideas for Disney's theme parks. Kachur hit the jackpot with her manager. Back in 2011, she had the idea of doing her Masters of Science in Creativity and Innovation at Buffalo State University to help with the work she was doing at Disney.

'There was one time when I was about halfway into the course where I was having a hard time with it', recalls Kachur. 'It was gruelling and I was getting tired. I had done the first year and I had finished the creative leadership portion. I felt confident in creative problem-solving methodology and I had learnt a few other innovation models, so I thought I was ready to move on.'

Kachur remembers her director's reaction. 'She was incredibly supportive but also encouraged me to see it through. She said to me, "You should stay with it. You need to finish this and you need to see it through".'

So Kachur picked herself up and ended up completing the course in 2014. 'Had I not finished the course, I wouldn't have been able to explore design thinking, which is critical to our work. We turned our focus to the Guest. We watched and listened. We asked: What are they doing? What are they saying? What unmet needs are we able to explore? How does our brand fit into their lifestyle? And most importantly, Why? It was design thinking that helped us put the Guest at the heart of the innovation process and allowed us to build holistic immersive retail experiences in a completely new way.'

★★★

There's a significant amount of research into the impact that managers have on teams and individuals with respect to creating a culture of innovation. Perhaps not surprisingly, studies have demonstrated that a team's overall view of its leader is strongly associated with their success in creative projects. In addition, individuals who feel that their manager is supportive perform more effectively on innovation projects.

> ... not surprisingly, studies have demonstrated that a team's overall view of its leader is strongly associated with their success in creative projects.

Professor Teresa Amabile suggests that the way in which managers support their teams falls into two categories of behaviour.

1 *Task-oriented behaviours* include activities that managers can perform to help provide clarity, resources and structure to people's roles. For example, task-oriented behaviours might include providing clarity on what a person's role is, helping employees to plan and structure projects, and providing people with the resources necessary to do their job well.

2 *Relationship-oriented behaviours* include being friendly and supportive to employees, being empathic, and showing consideration for individuals' feelings and welfare.

Amabile and some Harvard Business School colleagues were interested in delving further into how exactly managers' behaviours affected innovation performance. They were curious to understand whether employees' perceptions of their boss affected day-to-day creativity; which behaviours had a negative or positive impact; and what impact these perceptions had on innovation over time.

To investigate these questions, in the study 'Leader behaviors and the work environment for creativity' Amabile and her colleagues recruited 238 people working across three different industries—high-tech, chemicals, and consumer products. All employees were 'knowledge workers' and thus innovation played a key role in the success of what they did in their job. All participants were asked to keep a work diary, which consisted of answering a couple of questions at the end of every day. Specifically, they were asked:

1 *Briefly describe one event from today that stands out in your mind as relevant to the target project, your feelings about the project, your work on the project, your team's feelings about the project, or your team's work on the project.*

2 *Add anything else you would like to report today.*

Employees were also specifically asked how supportive their manager was that day. To assess creative output, at the end of every month all employees were asked to rate their own behaviour, and that of their peers, on their 'creative contribution to the project during the past month'.

After following these employees and their respective project teams for a period of between two and nine months (depending on the length of the project), Amabile crunched the results. As predicted, employees' perceptions of the supportiveness of their supervisor was significantly related to their innovation performance. The data also revealed the specific types of managerial behaviour that were perceived to be supportive, and the behaviour that was perceived to be non-supportive.

Positive behaviours fell into four categories.

1  *Supporting behaviours* included things such as actively supporting team members' actions and decisions, socialising with the team, disclosing personal information, and helping to reduce stress and negative emotions in their team. Essentially, managers who genuinely demonstrated empathy and emotional support for their team had a positive impact on creative performance.

2  *Monitoring behaviours* were not so much about keeping a really close eye on things, but rather being in regular contact with the team, providing useful feedback on work, offering to help when problems arose, and not being overly controlling.

3  *Recognising behaviours* were those through which positive behaviour was recognised both privately and publicly.

4  *Consulting behaviours* involved acting in a collaborative manner with the team by asking for their advice and ideas, and listening to their ideas and respecting them.

Overall, the positive behaviours can be classified into the original two categories that Amabile started with—task-related and relationship-related. For managers, keeping a check on both types of behaviour is important in getting the best out of teams.

On the flip side, there are behaviours that Amabile found led to a decrease in the perception of managers' supportiveness and a reduction in creative performance. These behaviours included failing to provide clarity on projects and not providing people with realistic deadlines; being overly controlling, micromanaging and providing non-constructive feedback; appearing disinterested in their team's work; and either creating problems and/or failing to solve problems when they arose.

While the study was not designed to show cause and effect, it is clear from the diary entries that there is a direct relationship between how managers behave and the good (or bad) outcomes they directly cause. For example, one employee who was part of the study says:

> At the working meeting [with a teammate and Sue, the team leader] ... the team changed from a 'Sue leading' to a 'three equals' format as the day progressed. This made everyone more outgoing, more ideas were discussed, and more progress was made.

Another employee wrote about the negative impact that a manager had on behaviour:

> I have this feeling that I'm not being utilised to my full potential — it's a shame that when I proactively seek work I'm given nothing or undemanding work.

These reactions are perhaps to be expected. I am sure many of us have been in similar situations—both with fantastic bosses who are inclusive, supportive, and help make our working lives easier and clearer; and with horrible bosses who micromanage, fail to provide meaningful feedback and don't seem to care about our well-being. What's important to recognise here is the significant impact these behaviours have on our ability to innovate.

So there are a couple of things to take away from this research. First, being a great manager involves building strong relationships with your team, and genuinely caring about people. Behaviours such as showing a real interest in people, disclosing personal information about yourself, demonstrating empathy and even socialising with your team all help to build a more supportive relationship.

But focusing on just the interpersonal aspects of management is not enough when it comes to driving innovation. The second factor to consider is task-related behaviours. Helping your team track their progress (without being a micromanager), providing feedback on work, seeking to make decisions in a consultative manner, setting appropriate goals, and helping to get rid of road blocks that are standing in the way of the team's success are all just as important in driving innovation.

Chapter 2 discusses the importance of autonomy, but it is also worth raising it here: it is one of the most important things managers can provide to support innovation. Professor Greg Oldham and his colleague Anne Cummings investigated the impact of controlling versus non-controlling managers on innovation output. They found that employees whose managers provided a great deal of autonomy (that is, were non-controlling) were significantly more innovative, produced more patent disclosures and were much less likely to leave the organisation. (See chapter 2 for more detail on this.)

Catherine Ramus, an assistant professor at the University of California (Santa Barbara) was interested in the impact of a manager's behaviour on employees' motivation to create and submit environmental innovations. Over three hundred employees from several large organisations headquartered in Europe were recruited for the research.

All participants were asked to describe the types of behaviours their manager displayed, and were also asked if they had ever developed an environmental initiative. The results showed that employees were much more likely to have developed an environmental innovation if they had a supportive manager. Specifically, when managers encouraged employees to present them with new ideas, provided feedback on their ideas, provided recognition for a job well done, and provided clarity around goals and expectations, employees were more likely to develop environmental innovations.

Ramus found that managers who were supportive of their employees innovating lifted the probability of an employee developing and promoting an environmental innovation from 34 per cent to up to 55 per cent.

Matthew Redmond, from George Mason University, and his colleagues were interested in looking at the effects of a leader's behaviour in a lab environment. Controlled manipulation of behaviour in this environment allowed researchers to see the effect this had on people's innovations. Ninety-six university students participated in the study. They were told that they had to solve a marketing problem (all students had completed at least one marketing subject, so had a good base level of knowledge).

Participants were instructed to assume the role of a marketing intern and were told that they had a manager, Mr Garr (who was played by an actor for the purposes of the experiment). The researchers were interested in the impact of the manager on building up a person's confidence in the marketing solutions generated. To manipulate this variable, Mr Garr told some participants that their performance on a battery of tests (which had been completed at the outset of the study) was well above average, while others were told their performance was about average.

The researchers found that when managers deliberately tried to enhance a person's confidence in their abilities, participants generated significantly more original (and better quality) solutions to the marketing problem. The researchers noted that enhancing a person's self-confidence helped them feel more motivated to complete the task well and to create more unique and novel solutions to problems. This aligns with research conducted by Professor Kimberly Jaussi, which demonstrated that merely telling someone they were creative led to them performing significantly better on a creative problem-solving task.

★★★

So we now know that increasing your team's confidence, providing task and role clarity, and building strong relationships with those you manage are critical factors in building a culture where innovation thrives. One final point to remember is that, as a manager, you should ensure that you spend enough time with your team to listen and support them with their innovations.

At Foursquare, something that founder and CEO Dennis Crowley takes very seriously is making himself accessible to every single employee. In Foursquare's 'main room', which functions as a dining hall, a table tennis area and an all-staff meeting room, one of the four walls is occupied by a very long blackboard. It is on this blackboard wall that people can sign up for 'office hours' with Crowley. Sessions are ten minutes long and are open to anyone who puts their name on the blackboard. Many sessions involve employees pitching ideas or wanting to bounce thoughts around with him. As simple as this idea sounds, it is a great way of demonstrating how accessible the company's leader is to employees, and how supportive leaders can be about listening to people's ideas and thoughts.

# KEY POINTS

- The amount of support around innovation that managers provide has a very significant effect on creating an innovation culture.

- As a manager, it is important to focus on both task-oriented behaviours and relationship-oriented behaviours to drive innovation in those you manage. Task-oriented behaviours include activities that managers can perform to help provide clarity, resources and structure to people's roles. Relationship-oriented behaviours include being friendly and supportive to employees, being empathic and showing consideration for individuals' feelings and welfare.

- Enhancing a person's confidence in their ability has a significant impact on innovation performance; so, as manager, consistently recognising great creative performance will have a very positive effect on driving innovation.

- Make sure you are accessible to your team, and set aside time to listen to their ideas in the first place.

# CHAPTER 8

# SENIOR LEADER SUPPORT

How not doing what's expected
can reap results

Derek O'Donnell is an energetic and passionate Irishman. Long before innovation was a buzzword, O'Donnell, a senior leader in the supply chain division, was convinced of its importance for Coca-Cola Amatil. He engaged executive sponsors and created and developed Coca-Cola Amatil's Innov8 program, which fosters a bottom-up approach to identifying great ideas from the organisation's 6000-odd employees. Eight years on, O'Donnell still plays a role in championing innovation.

One of O'Donnell's original intentions for Innov8 was to encourage as many people as possible to bring forward ideas, but not give the false promise that every idea would be implemented—so that focus on idea quality was maintained at the same pace as quantity of ideas. Getting this message out to the organisation was challenging, as staff worked in geographically spread out manufacturing plants and warehouses, and those working the night shift never really had the chance to speak to those in head office. Rather than just choosing the easy target of those in head office, O'Donnell made it his mission to ensure Innov8 was an inclusive program and that everyone, no matter what their role and no matter where in the business they worked, would be encouraged to participate in innovation.

O'Donnell recalls a time back in Innov8's first year when one of the Brisbane warehouse team leaders put forward an idea. The employee worked night shift and wasn't exposed to ongoing daytime discussions and activities, so didn't realise that the innovation he had suggested had actually already been implemented by another team in the business and was going to be launched within the month.

At this point O'Donnell could have just sent the employee an email. But instead, he took a different, more personal tack. 'I set the alarm for two o'clock in the morning and I phoned him up', recalls O'Donnell. 'I said, "Hi, it's Derek O'Donnell from head office. I just wanted to talk to you about your suggested innovation." There was this huge pregnant pause, because I'm not sure the employee had ever received a call from head office.'

'Should I clarify again why I'm calling?' O'Donnell asked.

The employee replied, 'I just can't believe you've called me'.

'Well, it's just about your innovation. It was a really great idea, but I just wanted to give you some context. We won't go ahead with it, but the reason why is because it actually is already in play and will be effective on your site in about four weeks.'

The employee said, 'You know what? I just really appreciate the fact that you've told me that, and you've called me'.

O'Donnell remembers the longer term impact that 2 am phone call had on the employee. 'Even though he'd received a rejection, he kept submitting lots of ideas into the program and became one of the program's biggest contributors and advocates. While innovation can often be seen as being about the ideas, it is just as important to treat people like adults and show respect for their views, which encourages them to become vibrant, consistent providers of fantastic ideas that can become business-improving innovations.'

★★★

When I was pregnant with my daughter, I would have regular catch-ups with one of my oldest girlfriends —someone I had known since we were five years old. Monique had four kids of her own (all under seven) and out of all my friends was the most 'expert' mum I knew. After all, she had gone through what I was about to go through four times and in fairly quick succession.

During one catch-up we were talking about all the things you had to book your child in for at birth—such as schools, childcare and sleep school.

'Sleep school?' I asked. I knew that I would experience extreme sleep deprivation, but I didn't think I needed to go to school to learn about it.

'Yes', Monique replied. 'For your baby. To teach your baby how to sleep.'

'I'll be fine!' I retorted. I had read all the books and I knew that as soon as Frankie (my daughter) came out of the womb, I would put her on a routine, and that would be that. Little did I know that the decision to go on a routine was not actually my choice. It was Frankie's. And she opted out.

When Frankie was eight weeks old, she had not slept for more than two hours in any given block. I think there might have been one time where she slept for three hours, but I was too sleep deprived to remember it. It

*(continued)*

felt as if all of the other mums in my mothers' group had babies who were already sleeping through the night (or at least sleeping for four or five hours in a row). That sounded like heaven. I picked up the phone and called Monique.

'Which sleep school was it that you recommended?'

The next day I booked in to see my GP, who got me on the waiting list for what Monique had said was one of the top sleep schools. Despite hearing horror stories about how the waiting list was 12 weeks long (which is an eternity when you have a non-sleeping baby), I was offered a place a few weeks later—when Frankie was three months old.

Sleep school changed our lives and was among the best five days I had in those first few months with Frankie. For the first time in three months I slept for six hours straight! I felt like a new woman. And Frankie was a little superstar at sleep school. She responded brilliantly to all the techniques we were taught, and lo and behold, we finally had a routine that worked for both of us.

Prior to checking in at sleep school I had read a few short accounts of other mums' experiences via a large Melbourne mothers Facebook group I was part of. I remember reading the accounts and thinking to myself, 'I wish there was more detail there—enough detail so that I could actually apply the techniques while waiting to be admitted to sleep school'.

So during Frankie's very first sleep at sleep school, I decided to start a blog. I made the decision that I would document my time at sleep school and everything I was learning, so that other mums who were on the waiting list, or who couldn't afford to go to sleep school, could benefit from these life-changing techniques. I also thought it would be a good way for me to remember everything I was learning—because there was so much to learn.

I bought a domain name (notanothermumblog.com), built a free blog through WordPress, and wrote my first post. I posted a link to the blog on the Melbourne mothers group in Facebook, and also sent a link to my own mothers' group, who were keen to find out what I learnt. I blogged every day of my five-day stay. When I checked my site visits at the end, it said 10 002. After posting a link to the blog in only two places, it had gone viral.

I kept writing the blog, journalling my experiences post–sleep school. It's all well and good for the techniques to work at sleep school when you are surrounded by amazing nurses, but we were all a bit nervous about going home and seeing if the success continued. Lo and behold, it did. After experiencing the results, I decided to make it my personal mission to educate even more people about these great techniques. The blog wasn't enough.

The next day, I contacted the CEO of the hospital that owned the sleep school. I told her that I wanted to turn my experience and the techniques into a book. She seemed excited enough about the idea to agree to meet with me so I could share my thoughts, but then ended the meeting by saying she would need to run the idea by Marketing and Legal.

I left the meeting feeling optimistic—after all, if the CEO was behind it, surely it was a done deal?

*(continued)*

Several weeks later, and after much chasing, the CEO finally got back to me. The answer was no. I asked why. She said that the sleep school didn't want to share their techniques with those who hadn't been to sleep school, and felt that doing so would reduce the number of enrolments—people would be able to read a book to learn about sleep school, rather than book in for the full-blown experience.

Now, I hope that you are feeling as shocked as I was when I heard this news. I obviously rebutted everything she said (didn't she know that books are an amazingly effective brand-builder and would definitely increase enrolments rather than decrease them? And hadn't she, a few weeks ago, complained that one of the biggest problems with the sleep school was that the waiting list was on average 12 weeks long…?).

I felt utterly frustrated by the whole experience. I had basically volunteered to write a book that would function as a brilliant marketing tool for them, and they declined because they didn't want to take the risk. And I felt disappointed that the leaders had not taken the risk and moved the idea forward.

It is not uncommon for senior leaders to play it safe when confronted with the choice of whether to support innovation. I recently worked with the Australian leadership team of a global technology company. While innovation was a strategic priority for the company globally, the Australian CEO was frightened of innovation because it meant taking a risk. And this fear permeated the business, which meant that employees were too nervous to do anything differently, because that was the message they were getting from the top.

★★★

Samuel Hunter and his colleagues Katrina Bedell and Michael Mumford found that the fifth most impactful variable in creating a culture of innovation is the perception that top-level management is truly supportive of innovation. In our own research at Inventium, we have found that one of the biggest differentiators between innovative versus non-innovative companies is the degree to which employees feel that senior leaders really understand what innovation means in a practical sense — as opposed to just paying lip-service to it.

Unfortunately, I find that there is a lot of lip-service paid to innovation. I am often asked to deliver keynotes on innovation at company conferences all over the world. The need for an innovation keynote can be triggered by all sorts of things: a company deciding that 'innovation' will be its theme for the year; innovation being a key strategic pillar of the company; or a CEO announcing to shareholders that the future is all about growth through innovation — and needing to back up that message with a relevant keynote speaker.

I find that these conferences fall into two categories:

1   those in which the leadership team is serious about innovation

2   those in which the leadership team is simply paying lip-service to a word that they don't even really understand.

I can tell I am in the company of leadership teams that fall into the first category when there is a clear strategy and plan of attack for how the organisation will approach innovation post-conference. For example, the leadership team will probably have set aside resources — in the form of money and time — to help people innovate. I recently delivered a keynote address for a global construction company, and at the conference they announced the appointment of five full-time Innovation Leads across their five different regions, in addition to a plan of attack for financially funding innovation. I knew they were serious about innovation.

In contrast, I get asked to speak at all sorts of conferences that have themes such as 'doing things differently', 'disrupt the future' or 'create, innovate, inspire'. When preparing my keynote I'll always have conversations with several leaders within the company and ask about their plans for innovation post-conference. And when I get answers such as 'We'll let the teams work it out' or 'We will leave it up to each individual to decide how they will apply your innovation lessons', I know that they need to learn more about innovation. While it's great for senior leadership teams to empower those below them, the plan falls down if the leadership team fails to provide direction, focus and resources. If they don't provide these things, then innovation will not happen.

★★★

There are many ways in which senior leaders can demonstrate their support for innovation. The most successful ways I have seen involve behaviours that truly symbolise their involvement in innovation — and that can almost become like folklore within the organisation.

> The most successful ways I have seen [for senior leaders to demonstrate their support for innovation] involve behaviours that truly symbolise their involvement in innovation.

One of the most powerful stories I heard was from Chad Dickerson, CEO of Etsy.

At the end of 2010, when Dickerson was CTO of Etsy, he decided to take a vacation to an island called Ocracoke, off the coast of North Carolina. In case you haven't heard of Ocracoke, it's a place where people holiday in the summer, mostly, and it can only be reached by ferry. In the winter, during the off-season, there are only about 700 residents.

'After making the decision to holiday in Ocracoke and relax over the holidays, I decided to look to see if there were any Etsy sellers on this remote island. It turned out there was, and her name was Mary', explained Dickerson.

'I sent Mary a message on Etsy and said, "Hey, this is probably going to sound strange but I'm holidaying in Ocracoke in a few weeks' time. I'm the CTO of Etsy and I'd love to meet up and talk to you about your experience, because it's always useful to learn from people who are selling on Etsy".'

Mary wrote back to Dickerson straightaway. 'The next thing I knew, we were out on the beach in her Jeep. She's a photographer and she was taking me along on her daily photography trip. There were dolphins in the water', says Dickerson. 'It was really, really beautiful.'

Dickerson goes on to explain, 'Spending time with Etsy sellers is really important to how we think about building Etsy. We have many sellers who work at Etsy. When we think about innovation and how we build the company, because Etsy is an online business with real-world activity, we try to embed ourselves in those environments'.

The learnings from the trip were obviously immense, but of even bigger impact was the signal the trip sent out to the organisation — that senior leaders are not just all talk about getting closer to customers and using that insight to drive innovation.

Another example of leaders encouraging innovation, and specifically taking a customer-centric approach, happened a few years ago when the leadership team at Etsy announced an initiative called Home for the Holidays. People who work at Etsy are mostly from all over the United States, and employees were given a stipend to have a meet-up with Etsy sellers in their hometown over the holidays.

'We had dozens of them', recalls Dickerson. 'We had meet-ups in Seattle, in Boston, and in many other cities. Employees invited Etsy sellers out to meet with them. Even just walking around Brooklyn [where Etsy's head office is located], we're always in contact with people who are using Etsy.'

★★★

Getting involved in innovation in a hands-on way as Dickerson does is one of the most powerful things leaders can do to create a culture of innovation. In a six-year research study Professor Jeff Dyer, from Brigham Young University, and his colleagues surveyed more than 3500 people, including senior executives at a wide range of companies, and individuals who had started innovative companies or invented a new product. The researchers divided this large group of people into those who were leaders at highly innovative companies, and those who were leaders at non-innovative companies.

> Getting involved in innovation in a hands-on way … is one of the most powerful things leaders can do to create a culture of innovation.

When analysing the types of behaviours these leaders regularly engaged in, it became clear that the differences were stark. Leaders at the non-innovative companies felt it was their job to delegate or facilitate innovation. Instead of getting their hands dirty and going out and speaking to customers and prototyping and testing ideas, they preferred to get others to do the work.

In contrast, leaders at innovative companies saw innovation squarely as their job. They could be found speaking with a broad range of people to elicit different views on ideas they were thinking of, they were getting out of the office and testing their prototypes with different people and asking lots of questions and getting lots of feedback.

And these differences were not small. Leaders (including several CEOs) at innovative companies spent 50 per cent more time on what the researchers termed 'discovery activities' than their counterparts at non-innovative organisations. Discovery activities included things such as making links between seemingly disparate pieces of information, asking questions and challenging assumptions, observing customers and their behaviour, trying out new ideas and prototypes, and testing ideas through a diverse range of networks.

★★★

Researchers have questioned whether support from senior leaders is more critical for incremental, exploitative innovation, or for breakthrough and explorative types of innovation. Verena Mueller, from Justus Liebig University, and her colleagues set out to explore this very question.

In a meta-analysis consisting of 46 studies and over 12 000 participants, they examined the impact of leadership style on various innovation outputs. Through their analysis, they found that companies that were more centralised and had stronger, more decisive leadership actually performed significantly better when it came to producing successful breakthrough innovations. The researchers explained it thus: 'As high-risk projects, exploratory innovations need the support of a powerful top management that pursues them despite the potential resistance of employees and middle managers because of potential cannibalisation effects'. In contrast, this style of management is not especially impactful on lower-risk, incremental innovations.

Mike Finch, the joint CEO and artistic director of Circus Oz, personifies the type of hands-on innovative leader that Dyer described. 'If I had a choice', jokes Finch, 'creating new innovations is all I would do!' One example of Finch's discovery skills in action is demonstrated in a story about hot air balloons.

Something you might not have known about hot air balloons is that, at a certain age, they get too dangerous to fly because they start to rot. What then happens is that the top half of the balloon gets cut off, and it gets written off. Fortuitously, Circus Oz's props designer, Dave Murphy, got his hands on a half-balloon. Finch recalls, 'Dave showed it to me and said "let's have a play", so we just played for a whole day—just me and him—blowing up the top half of a hot air balloon and filling the entire rehearsal space. If you just put it on the ground and blow air under it with a blower, it'll inflate and just sit there. The weight of the fabric seals it to the ground.

'One of the most spectacular things we found was that if you just stand on one side of it and just give it a hard tug down, the entire thing starts to roll back like an eyelid. It doesn't collapse because the air stays and it just rolls all the way back. Then another thing you can do is if there's a string hanging from the centre when it's inflated, you can just pull the string down and the whole thing just falls in a pile of fabric in the centre.'

The possibilities for the hot air balloon percolated in Mike's head for over a decade. Every so often he would drag the balloon back out. Finch describes the company's reaction: 'People would be like, "Oh, no. Here's Mike's balloon again"'.

Then finally, about three years ago, the balloon experiments came into their own. Finch had his own balloon parachute made, which was a bit smaller than the real deal and all white. For the opening of the show, the very first image was of the balloon as a big white dome onstage. When the audience was seated, Finch and his team used the eyeball roll-back technique to reveal the entire band underneath.

The finale of the show looped back around to the balloon. Finch says, 'We used the dome effect of the balloon as the finale of the show and we actually turned it into a dress. We created this effect with one of our performers, Sarah Wood. Her character in the show was a diva and she's trying to sing all through the show, and then right at the end she rises up above the stage in this long, white dress. She goes right up to the roof, and then the dress starts to inflate and then people pull it up until she's in a giant hoop-skirt dress that is the dome. Then, at the very end, the music peaks, she goes down through the centre, into the dress and then the whole dress does that thing when you pull the string and it disappears in on itself. The whole thing sucks into this box and it's just her standing in her underwear and she jumps into the box and goes, "Tah-dah!" It's the end of the show. The whole show's sucked in.'

# KEY POINTS

- If you are a senior leader, make sure that you see your role as actually *doing* innovation, as opposed to just delegating it to other people.

- As a leader, think about behaviours you can engage in that symbolise your commitment to, and support of innovation.

- Leaders at highly innovative companies engage in discovery activities significantly more often than leaders at non-innovative organisations. Discovery activities include making links between seemingly disconnected pieces of information, asking questions, challenging assumptions, observing customers, testing prototypes and speaking to a diverse range of networks about innovations.

- When pursuing breakthrough and disruptive types of innovation, having a centralised and decisive senior leadership team is critical in making sure that projects that can seem high-risk actually see the light of day.

# CHAPTER 9

# RESOURCING

## In for a penny, but not necessarily in for a pound

In 2005 the management team at Intuit was studying the likes of Google and 3M, both of which famously implemented a concept called 20% Time, in which employees were allowed to spend 20 per cent of their time at work on self-set innovation projects. The research had suggested that this initiative had led to greater employee engagement. Inspired by these stories, Intuit's CTO began asking several leaders within the business, 'Who wants to experiment with a program like this?'

Hugh Molotsi worked in the Small Business group at Intuit at the time. 'Our product development leader responded to the call saying, "Yes. We'll experiment". We launched a 10 per cent program we ended up calling 'Unstructured Time' in the Small Business group and decided that we would run it for a year and report out to the rest of the company how it was going. It was almost immediately so successful that a couple of other business units just sort of jumped in and said "Yeah, we're going to do it, too".'

By 2008 Intuit's newly anointed CEO Brad Smith declared that Unstructured Time was for everybody.

It's all well and good to say to every employee 'spend half a day a week working on whatever you like', but it's another thing to consider how that works practically, on a day-to-day basis. For example, do employees need to get approval for what they work on in this self-set time?

'The intent is that there's no approval needed', explains Molotsi. 'We say we'd like employees to tell their managers what they're working on but that's more just to create awareness. Maybe a manager can help connect with other people, but the whole point of the program is it's meant to be autonomous. This is something the employee's interested in. Hence, we see a wide range of uses.'

At Intuit, Molotsi estimates that about half of the people who take advantage of Unstructured Time use it to solve customer problems. Then there are a little more than a quarter who spend it on process improvements — things that have to do with work but that present opportunities to make it more efficient and save time. The remainder use the time for their own personal development, such as learning a new skill.

'People do aggregate the time and use it in blocks', Molotsi says. 'Because we found that, especially for the type of work we do, it's often more realistic to be able to put a few days together where you can work on the problem continuously versus just four hours a week. Most people use it by saving up the time and using it in continuous blocks.'

'We ... want to make sure that people who are interested in Unstructured Time don't face any blockers or issues that prevent them from using it.'
Hugh Molotsi

Molotsi's team surveys people monthly through a pop-up questionnaire on the company's intranet that asks 'Have you used Unstructured Time in the last month?' Results show that in any given month, 13 to 15 per cent of employees have used it, which translates to around half of the company using Unstructured Time over the course of a year.

'We think if we have half the employees using Unstructured Time, that's a good goal', says Molotsi, who admits that Unstructured Time is not for everyone. 'To be honest, some people have this sentiment that "Look, I'm just here to do the job I'm assigned and then go home". We don't feel like we want to twist people's arms to say "No. Do Unstructured Time". We simply want to make sure that people who are interested in Unstructured Time don't face any blockers or issues that prevent them from using it.'

★★★

In 2012, LinkedIn initiated its own take on the notion of giving employees unstructured time to develop ideas—the [in]cubator program. Prior to this program launching, LinkedIn, like many other companies, had held regular hack days. Hack days were held once a month, on a Friday, and provided people with time to work on anything they chose. The idea for the [in]cubator program came from a group of hack day regulars who felt there was a limit to what could realistically be created in a day. The solution was giving employees up to 90 consecutive days to work on self-set innovation projects. However—there was a catch. Employees only got the full 90 days if they successfully passed several checkpoints along the way.

In practice, the [in]cubator program allows people to pitch their ideas to an executive team once a quarter. If accepted, the team behind the idea gets 30 days to work on their project and build a prototype. Progress is reviewed at the 30-day mark and if the project still shows promise, another 30 days is awarded. The 60-day mark is the final checkpoint, and teams that are still making good progress are awarded another 30 days. In addition, LinkedIn founder Reid Hoffman provides mentoring to teams along the way.

★★★

While being given a set time to be able to innovate is fantastic in theory, another issue that companies must contend with when offering such a system is that most of us are not natural-born innovators. And even if we are, it's a skill set that, unfortunately, the education system knocks out of us. What we know from science is that the skills to become an effective innovator can be learned. For organisations this means that resourcing the people side of innovation isn't just about giving people time, but also about ensuring that people have the skills to innovate.

> Resourcing the people side of innovation isn't just about giving people time, but also about ensuring that people have the skills to innovate.

'One of the things we do at Intuit to make sure everybody can effectively innovate is we teach everybody two core competencies', explains Molotsi. 'We teach something we call CDI, which is Customer-Driven Innovation. We also teach something called D for D, which is Design for Delight—our version of design thinking, which we teach to every employee. This way, we try and arm employees with effective approaches to innovation—how to make sure your solution is really solving a problem. In addition to that, we have an innovation catalyst program and people can sign up to be trained to be innovation catalysts. When they do that, they spend 20 per cent of their time helping other employees practise Design for Delight. We have over two hundred employees who have trained to be innovation catalysts.'

Most large organisations that are serious about innovation have some form of innovation catalysts or 'champions'. At Pfizer there are 500 innovation champions who dedicate 10 to 15 per cent of their time to helping facilitate and coach people through the innovation process. Recruiting these champions provided some important learning. For the first batch of champions, leaders nominated high performers to whom they wanted to give new opportunities. However, to their surprise, it turned out that the people who really thrived in this role were not necessarily those 'high performers'.

Vice President of Worldwide Innovation, Wendy Mayer explains. 'What we found was that the people that were really destined for this role were people who were really passionate about innovation. These were people who wanted to be involved and understand what business challenges were happening across the organisation. They loved the role of being a facilitator and helping to lead sessions and work with the teams in helping to develop solutions.'

In 2015 the innovation champion recruitment process evolved to allow people to nominate themselves and then go to their managers to get confirmation that they would be comfortable with the time commitment. Mayer says, 'Through using this new approach, the engagement has been unbelievable. We've really gotten it right in terms of finding people that have a passion. And for them, the 10 to 15 per cent commitment isn't a burden. It's a pleasure'.

Research certainly backs up the idea that great innovation can come from self-set time. In one study, Pilar Martín, from the University of Zaragoza, and her colleagues set out to investigate the impact of having time to work on innovation outcomes. The researchers recruited 244 employees from Spanish companies in the tile sector. These employees were asked questions such as whether they were able to determine which tasks they work on day to day, the amount of work they did every day, and whether their role provided them with the opportunity to apply their specific skill set. Employees were also asked about their own innovation output—specifically, how often they try out new ideas when engaged at work.

The researchers found that employees who felt as if they had greater resources available to do their job—including control over how they used their time and the ability to apply their specific skill set to their role—engaged in innovative behaviours far more frequently than those who felt they had a lack of resources.

★★★

When it comes to the monetary side of innovation, I tend to come across two very common problems in the consulting work I do at Inventium. The first is companies who over-resource innovation. This problem generally springs from executives who believe that to produce big innovations, you need to spend big bucks. And what tends to happen with innovation projects is that if they don't seem to be working or attracting enough customers initially, the instinct is to simply throw more money at them. And, unfortunately, this cycle tends to repeat itself.

The other problem I see around funding innovation is the complete lack of it. I regularly encounter organisations that talk about how innovation is at the core of what they do, but have no money set aside to test and prototype ideas, and scale the ones that show promise.

One of the projects that Inventium works on annually is the *BRW* Most Innovative Companies list—Australia's premier list that ranks the nation's most innovative organisations. Inventium does the judging and analysis work that goes into compiling the list; we receive hundreds of entries every year, and each entrant must complete Inventium's Innovation Audit (a tool for measuring how an organisation is performing on the key drivers of innovation). One of the areas the Innovation Audit looks at is resourcing. In this year's analysis we found that at the poorest performing companies, 50 per cent of employees said that little or no resources were dedicated to innovation. This statistic blows my mind, given that organisations that enter the awards surely feel they are committed to innovation. Clearly there are many organisations out there that truly believe they can grow through innovation without committing any time or money to the cause.

While a successful innovation program does indeed require money, organisations need to find a middle ground. The solution is microfunding (otherwise known as seed funding), an approach that gained a lot of traction and publicity thanks to Paul Graham and three of his colleagues.

Back in 2005 Graham had an idea that was to turn traditional venture capital notions on their head. Rather than betting big and on fewer investments, he felt it would make much more sense to bet small and on a greater number of investments—and, in addition, to fund hackers rather than suits. To bring these thoughts to fruition, Graham and his partner Jessica Livingston decided to start Y Combinator; and, in conjunction with Trevor Blackwell and Robert Morris, the new company was born.

A lot of people (including Graham himself) didn't take Y Combinator hugely seriously at first. Graham writes about the early days:

> When people came to YC to speak at the dinners that first summer, they came in the spirit of someone coming to address a boy scout troop. By the time they left the building, they were all saying some variant of 'Wow, these companies might actually succeed'.

The model behind Y Combinator, which has evolved over the last ten years, is essentially to bet small and bet on many. Twice a year Y Combinator opens its doors to start-ups in search of support. Up until a couple of years ago (its funding model has now changed), Y Combinator would invest an average of US$18 000 in early-stage start-ups and invite them to relocate to Silicon Valley for three months of mentoring, experimenting and iterating. The three-month period was designed to be used to essentially build, ship and learn.

Y Combinator has invested in some of the most successful start-ups on the planet, including Dropbox, Airbnb, Reddit, Stripe and Weebly. The total market capitalisation of all Y Combinator companies is more than $30 billion.

This microfunding approach has been adopted by large organisations as a way to help diversify innovation investments and, by doing so, help mitigate the inherent risk in funding innovation. In Australia, Deloitte provides $10 000 of microfunding for ideas the firm sees as showing promise. Microfunding decisions are made by the Innovation Council, a group made up of partners within Deloitte who meet once a month. Teams that are given the go-ahead and $10 000 are expected to present back to the Innovation Council within a couple of months to report on progress. And if progress is looking good, more money is invested.

Adobe has another take on microfunding: its Kickboxes. While the term may conjure up images of employees taking to the boxing ring at work, the name came from an innovation kit, called the Kickbox, that is given to any Adobe employee who asks for one. A Kickbox is a small, red box that contains everything an employee would need to identify an opportunity to solve, generate solutions, prototype those solutions and ultimately test new ideas. In addition to a Starbucks voucher and a chocolate bar (coffee and chocolate being two essential food groups for innovators), the box contains guidance on how to successfully innovate, and a $1000 pre-paid credit card.

Vice President of Creativity at Adobe and the creator of the Kickbox Mark Randall, was inspired by the energy of Silicon Valley hackathons, but wanted to create something that was more scalable, and also more tangible to all employees (not just programmers). Like the Y Combinator approach, the Kickbox program is a way of placing thousands of small bets rather than just a few big ones. Any employee is able to request a Kickbox, and their manager is unable to veto the request. More than a thousand Kickboxes were distributed in the program's first two years, and several successful innovations have shipped as a result.

Adobe has released its Kickbox innovation process under a Creative Commons license, so it's available and free for anyone to use. The idea has caught on at many organisations around the world. In Australia, Nestlé created its own version, called the Red Box program. Fifty employees in the food division were given a red box that contained instructions on the 'five steps to innovate' and \$500 to be spent on testing the concept. Employees had five weeks to innovate, and the program culminated in people pitching their idea to a Dragons' Den–style panel comprising several senior leaders and some external parties. Of the ideas that were pitched, three were given a blue box—which equated to further funding for the most promising innovations. All of these ideas are now moving forward and have the potential to have a significant impact on the business.

During the five-week campaign, Head of Innovation for Nestlé Australia Mariah Monaghan, noticed something interesting. 'We found that while the \$500 played a really important role, it wasn't so much around people actually spending it, but rather in people feeling empowered because it was there. And instead of spending money, the tight constraints actually encouraged people to tap into networks within the Nestlé business—both within Australia and globally.'

Commonwealth Bank of Australia took the Kickbox idea a step further with CANapult, a can that helps launch ideas into action and has been gamified to encourage participation. When an employee comes forward with an idea, they are sent a CANapult can, which contains a handwritten note from an executive and a stack of tools to help define, test and pitch their idea. The CANapult process is broken into six stages, all of which are described within the kit, to help people identify if their idea is worth pursuing and how they can develop it. The six steps are:

1   Define the idea – what is it and what it will do.

2   Discover what customers think of their idea.

3   Create a prototype.

4   Validate the idea through the Business Model Canvas.

5   Experiment and test.

6   Pitch the idea to key stakeholders for funding to move forward.

One of the defining features of CANapult is that it gamifies the innovation process. 'As people progress through each stage', explains

Head of Innovation Lab at Commonwealth Bank of Australia Tiziana Bianco, 'they are eligible for more rewards and funding, with a total of up to $650 per idea'. The internal innovation team are on hand to support all participants and, in addition, people are assigned a 'Buddy' from within the business who is going through the same journey, allowing them to share experiences.

'We get a lot of ideas in the bank', explains Bianco. 'This process enables people to understand what it actually takes to make innovation happen.'

The next phase for CANapult is to take the program outside the bank, and invite customers and suppliers to co-create ideas.

★★★

Professor Riitta Katila from Stanford University led a study to examine the impact of a lack of financial resources on innovation. In what was a unique methodology, Katila tracked 1397 invention patents that had come from the Massachusetts Institute of Technology between 1980 and 1996. She then looked at how many attempts there had been by companies to licence and commercialise these inventions—a total of 964. The researchers followed each of these innovation attempts until the company had commercialised the product (that is, launched the product for sale and started to make money), terminated the licence for the patent, or the observation period of the research had ended. Only 197 of the inventions had been commercialised by the end of the research period.

Katila also applied several measures to each of the companies that had commercialised, or failed to commercialise, the inventions. She looked at the newness of the firm (measured by whether it was in existence prior to licensing the patent); the competitiveness of the industry (measured by the number of firms operating); the manufacturing intensity (calculated by dividing the dollar value of manufacturing the product by the dollar value of shipments); and the size of the market (based on the annual dollar value of shipments).

In her analysis, Katila paid special attention to these variables, especially how new the firm was, given this would indicate whether a lack of financial resources affected a company's ability to commercialise its innovation. It was found that new firms with a lack of financial resources were actually more likely to be successful with their innovation efforts in markets that had a greater number of competitors. New firms were also more likely to do well in smaller markets, and also in those markets that were less manufacturing-intensive.

Essentially, what this study demonstrates is that you don't need to be rich in financial terms to perform well with respect to innovation. And while this study was focused on the impact of a lack of financial resources on new market entrants, the lesson for established companies is that you don't need to throw lots of money at innovations in order to ensure their success—especially when the market is highly competitive, or is smaller, or has lower manufacturing intensity.

## KEY POINTS

- Setting aside time and money for innovation is critical to creating an innovation culture.

- Consider giving employees self-set time to innovate—but also provide them with the training to be effective innovators. (Innovation is a learned skill.)

- Avoid the trap of over- or under-resourcing innovation. Instead, provide microfunding—small amounts of money given to a large number of innovations that show promise.

- Consider creating your own version of a Kickbox and taking microfunding to the masses.

# CHAPTER 10

# GOAL CLARITY

## Why blue-sky thinking is for the birds—it's an innovation killer

One of the biggest problems I encounter through the work I do at Inventium is 'blue-sky thinking'. You may be reading this and thinking, 'But I thought blue-sky thinking was a good thing. In fact, I participated in a blue-sky workshop just last month!' I hear this kind of thing a lot and I cringe when I hear it. Blue-sky workshops, where there is not a set goal or challenge—just a bunch of people sitting in a room being asked to come up with the next big thing for their industry—are a huge waste of time. Asking people to go blue-sky when it comes to innovation is like playing darts without a dartboard: you simply don't know where to aim. And while you may have a great time in the idea-generation workshop and feel really excited, ultimately you end up with a lot of ideas that collect dust on someone's desk and never see the light of day.

Another version of blue-sky thinking workshops occurs when organisations implement idea management software (a fancy phrase for an online suggestion box) and open it up to all employees to suggest absolutely any idea. I have seen this happen countless times and what inevitably happens—in the absence of clear challenges to solve—is that the innovation team will receive a stack of ideas. Hundreds, if not thousands. And the team sits around scratching their heads wondering a) how to give feedback about all these ideas and b) how to make decisions on which ones to implement. And the truth is, both of these questions are very difficult to answer. It is challenging to give feedback about ideas when you don't know what problem they are trying to solve. Likewise, it is almost impossible to make decisions about ideas when there is no set challenge or opportunity against which you can evaluate it.

Any decent innovation process needs to start with clear goals. At Inventium we call these Innovation Missions. Innovation Missions provide broad but focused opportunities that the organisation can look to pursue. Some of these missions will be focused on improving the core business (that is, on incremental innovation). Other missions will be focused on innovation that is more breakthrough or disruptive.

> Any decent innovation process needs to start with clear goals.

As well as the bigger organisation-wide goals, ensuring that teams and individuals are clear on the goals relating to the projects they are working on is critical in building a culture of innovation. There is decades' worth of research into goal setting and productivity, but there's also a smaller body of research into the effect of goal setting on innovation projects. At first glance, you might think that goal setting and innovation cannot co-exist, as innovation projects are by their very nature full of ambiguity and uncertainty. Martin Hoegl from Bocconi University set out to investigate this topic further.

Hoegl recruited 575 employees and managers from a total of 145 different software development teams in Germany. Each person was interviewed and asked several questions about the types of goals that they were set for an innovation project on which they were currently working. Questions included whether the goals were clear and comprehensive, whether the customer needs were clear, whether the manager had been clear in communicating his or her goals, and whether the goals had remained stable over the course of the project. They were also asked about how effectively their team worked together. The innovation project outcomes were then assessed for the technical quality of the software solutions and the efficiency of the projects, with respect to their being completed on time and on budget.

Hoegl found that goal setting had a significant impact on both quality and efficiency of project outcomes. But he also found that when teams had effective ways of working together, the relationship between goal setting and project outcomes was even stronger. It is important for managers to note that while goal setting is an important aspect of enhancing project outcomes with respect to innovation, the effects will be much stronger when the team works together effectively and communicates well.

★★★

Once you have organisation-wide missions in place and ensure that teams also have clear goals, it's time to start work on achieving them. However, it is surprisingly easy for employees to lose motivation somewhere along the journey. Missions, in particular, are huge goals and can take months, if not years, to achieve. Conventional 'motivational gurus' talk a lot about the importance of clear goals to help motivate—but these clear goals will only motivate people for so long. There is a crucial ingredient that you need to add to the mix to ensure motivation is maintained.

This critical ingredient is outlined in *The Progress Principle* by Teresa Amabile and Steven Kramer. One of the challenges of research is creating experimental conditions that are as close to real life as possible. Amabile and Kramer came up with a creative way to do this, by asking employees to complete daily work diaries. The study recruited people from 26 different project teams working across seven organisations—in total, 238 employees. The project teams had a diverse range of pursuits, from creating kitchen gadgets through to solving IT problems for a hotel chain. The commonality across projects was that they all required a strong element of innovation for their success.

Goal clarity

At the end of every day for four months, the 238 employees were emailed a survey to complete. The survey asked them about their work environment, their mood, events that stood out in their mind about the day, and their level of motivation. This resulted in a total of around 12 000 diary entries to analyse.

One of the questions Amabile and Kramer asked when analysing the data was, what were the differences between people's best days (based on how they were feeling and their levels of motivation) and their worst? The results were striking.

The number one difference between people's best and worst days was whether they took steps forward on their project, or took steps backwards. In other words, feeling a sense of progress was the most motivating factor in people's lives. On people's best days, 76 per cent had taken a step forward. In contrast, on their worst days, 67 per cent reported having a setback.

While research results can often seem obvious with the benefit of hindsight, Amabile and Kramer actually went out to 669 managers from a range of companies across the world and asked them what had the biggest impact on employee motivation. Managers were given five factors to choose from: making progress, receiving recognition, receiving incentives, having clear goals, and interpersonal support. Managers had to rank these five factors from the most impactful through to the least impactful. The majority of managers ranked 'receiving recognition for good work' as the most motivating factor, while only 5 per cent of managers said that 'making progress' was most motivating.

Another surprising factor about the research is that the progress that people reported making was generally quite small. For example, one participant, Tom, who was working on a complex billing problem, described one of his steps forward:

*I smashed that bug that's been frustrating me for almost a calendar week. That may not be an event to you, but I live a very drab life, so I'm all hyped. No one really knows about it; three of the team [members who] would be involved are out today—so I have to sit here rejoicing in my solitary smugness.*

The one caveat attached to the motivating power of progress is that the progress needs to come from doing meaningful work. If, for example, you are working in a job that bores you to tears and holds no sense of challenge or meaning for you, then you could make all the progress in the world but fail to become more engaged and motivated.

There are several things to consider when applying the 'progress principle':

- Rather than just setting big goals and milestones in relation to projects on which teams and individuals are working, set some smaller goals too. Setting these smaller goals will help people to identify their progress more clearly.

- Create a 'progress board' to help people visualise the progress they are making. This could be a central whiteboard that sits front and centre. At Inventium, we have created progress visuals for all sorts of projects. One confidential project involved the team achieving 200 'micro-wins' (we called these 'cherries', as our code name) so we created a grid chart with 200 boxes and every time someone had a micro-win, that person put up a cherry sticker. And when we hit certain milestones, such as 50 or 100 cherries, we would have a themed celebration, such as an afternoon tea of cherry pie, or chocolate-and-cherry ice cream. (We are very motivated by food.)

- Too often we only celebrate the big wins. Instead, take time out to celebrate the small wins that signal progress (in case people are oblivious to the progress they are actually making). Just like the cherry pies that we got for the team, think about how you can celebrate the day-to-day progress that you or your team make.

So far this chapter has looked at organisation-wide and team goals, but the other way to think about goal setting is in the context of individuals. Silvia da Costa, from the University of the Basque Country, and her colleagues reviewed several meta-analyses. The researchers examined the difference in innovation performance between people who were clear on both organisational objectives and objectives for their own role, compared with people who worked in environments where there was low clarity. The researchers found that 54 per cent of people who were clear on objectives (both organisation-wide and individual) demonstrated above-average creativity and innovation in their performance. In contrast, only 46 per cent of people who did not have this clarity showed above-average innovativeness.

Christine Gilroy, group general manager of innovation at property company Mirvac, has placed a deliberate focus on setting clear individual goals and key performance indicators (KPIs) around innovation. 'If you go back five to ten years at Mirvac', says Gilroy, 'innovation was something that happened but was left to chance and was quite reactive. We were good at reactive innovation—when we had a problem, people would come up with fantastic solutions, but we lacked a strategic approach to innovation. We hadn't stepped back and looked at the full universe of opportunities or challenges and decided where we wanted to focus'.

Mirvac's company-wide innovation program Hatch was launched in 2014. One of the components of the program, which provides a more proactive and strategic approach to innovation, is that the executive leadership team all have KPIs for innovation. In addition, the program's innovation champions all have a KPI around innovation, as do their managers. 'When the program becomes more mature, the aim is that every person in the organisation will have a KPI for innovation', explains Gilroy.

The performance of Mirvac's innovation champions is measured by their response to the question 'Give examples where you have added value to your Innovation Mission [a business challenge that the champion has been tasked with helping to solve] and the business by using the Hatch methodologies and innovation process'. All members of the executive leadership team have the KPI of enabling their team to contribute to innovation at Mirvac. The KPI is measured by people providing examples of supporting or enabling their team to achieve innovation objectives. Managers of innovation champions are also measured on this KPI to ensure they support and encourage their champion to contribute to innovation at Mirvac.

And if the idea of setting formal KPIs across your entire leadership team, innovation champions and managers of innovation champions feels like a huge leap, you could use an approach that one of our clients tried as a gentler start to embracing innovation KPIs. This particular client, a food manufacturer, decided to start with qualitative KPIs. Every six months, every single person in the R&D team was asked to answer two questions:

1   What ideas have you contributed that have made a difference?

2   How have you collaborated with others to build ideas?

Having a very clear and overt focus on innovation has meant that innovative behaviours have become more frequent and innovation is kept at the forefront of people's awareness — all through asking two very simple questions.

# KEY POINTS

- Rather than going blue-sky with your innovation efforts, leaders need to set clear organisation-wide goals to keep people's efforts focused and effective.

- Rather than just setting big goals and milestones in relation to projects on which teams and individuals are working, set some smaller goals too to help people feel a regular sense of progress. Consider making a progress board to demonstrate progress visually, and take time to celebrate smaller wins as well as bigger ones.

- Setting team goals has been shown to increase the effectiveness and efficiency of innovation project outcomes, so spend time making sure teams have clear goals.

- Consider setting innovation KPIs or other individual goals so that everyone in the organisation has clarity around how they contribute to the organisation's innovation efforts.

# PART IV
# ORGANISATION-
# LEVEL
# FACTORS

This final section of the book focuses on the variables that span the organisation as a whole. That is, these are elements that need to be present at not just an individual or team or leader level, but rather need to be ingrained into all parts and levels of a company. These variables are often the hardest ones to get right, given they need to be implemented across an entire company. However, they can also be some of the most powerful drivers of an innovation culture.

Having a culture that promotes risk-taking and flexibility is one of the most critical drivers of an innovation culture — but in large organisations it tends to be the variable that people struggle with the most. As a general rule, the larger the organisation, the less open it is to taking risks. There are several reasons why this happens, from red tape and bureaucracy (which of course tends to be rife within large organisations), through to the way accountabilities are set. Chapter 11 explores several ways that organisations can promote risk-taking without compromising their safety or security.

An organisation in which people feel a strong sense of togetherness is critical for creating a culture of innovation. Indeed, in their study 'Climate for creativity: A quantitative review', Samuel Hunter and his colleagues Katrina Bedell and Michael Mumford revealed this variable to have the single biggest impact on creating a culture of innovation. Chapter 12 explains what it actually means to have a cohesive culture, and ways in which you can create one at your organisation.

Chapter 13 looks at the importance of people feeling as if they, personally, have permission to take an active role in driving innovation. This chapter explores the notion of democratising innovation, and describes the circumstances in which this has been shown to be an effective driver of innovation.

Finally, chapter 14 explores the impact of the physical environment on creating a culture where innovation thrives. This chapter covers the latest research into the physical work environment and the attributes that have been shown to create, rather than kill, innovation and productivity.

# CHAPTER 11
# RISK-TAKING

## Failing for success

In *Apollo 13*, the 1995 movie about the ill-fated moon landing mission, NASA Flight Director Gene Krantz (played by Ed Harris), is talking to his team about the necessity of finding a way to preserve energy in the space shuttle. Members of the team are telling him that there are only enough amps to power the shuttle for 16 hours. Krantz responds by telling the team that they have never lost an American in space and they are not going to lose one under his watch. 'Failure is not an option', Harris memorably states. And while Krantz never actually said this line in real life, it stuck with him and became the title of his autobiography five years later.

The notion of failure being unacceptable is one I have found resonates with many organisations. Failure is generally thought of as a dirty word, and something that gets swept under the carpet when it does rear its ugly head. But being able to acknowledge and learn from failure is a huge part of building a culture where risk-taking is tolerated, and it is a concept that Engineers Without Borders (EWB) is very familiar with.

EWB is a not-for-profit organisation that supports social innovations that can help end global poverty and inequality. Its projects include the Run to End Poverty event, which is a fundraiser for various projects; Rent to Own, which makes it possible for entrepreneurs in rural Zambia to own new equipment through making regular 'rental' payments over a period of time; and Voto Mobile, which is a web-based platform that makes it easy to give citizens of Ghana a voice in policy creation and social change.

One of the particularly groundbreaking pursuits of EWB came about through internal conversations about how the organisation claimed to be humble yet didn't talk about all the ideas and ventures that were failures. As a result of this contradiction, 2008 saw the birth of the first *Failure Report*. Just like EWB's annual reports, the *Failure Report* is now published every year and is available for public download via the EWB website at www.ewb.ca. It's a relatively lengthy publication that details all of the year's failures. Each story published in the report talks about the intentions behind the project, what happened and (most importantly) the lessons learnt.

EWB's first *Failure Report* was seen as groundbreaking within the development sector which, like many other sectors, had traditionally swept failure under the carpet. The *Failure Report* was one of the sector's first steps towards making failure okay. A couple of years later, in 2011, EWB took the idea a step further and created a website called Admitting Failure (www.admittingfailure.org). Ashley Good, the leader behind the Admitting Failure venture and also the editor of the *Failure Report*, explains, 'There was a reason no one in the sector was talking about their failures already: development work is largely donor-driven and donors tend to stop funding people and projects that fail'. The purpose of the site is to encourage other development organisations to share what isn't working so that others can learn from their mistakes.

Several years on, the site is filled with stories. Marilyn McHarg, executive director of Médecins Sans Frontières, talks about the time she was supervising operations in Iraq and her team had arrived underprepared to treat the types of illnesses they were presented with. At the end of her story McHarg shares the learnings she took from the situation. A volunteer called Kelly Anderson tells the story of trying to help an orphanage in Haiti by providing them with a $700 water filter. After Anderson left, the filter was locked away in a closet because the orphanage staff were afraid it would be stolen—and hence it was never used to provide clean water for the children. And then one day, it was stolen.

★★★

When I tell people who work in the for-profit sector about this idea of sharing failures, the first response I get is that it would never work in their industry. However, I am not sure this is the case. Certainly, in Silicon Valley people talk about failure as being a rite of passage. FailCon, a conference that launched in San Francisco in 2009 and quickly went global, gathers thousands of technology entrepreneurs, start-up founders, investors and developers together to share their stories of failure. People from Google, Yammer, Uber and many other successful companies have all taken the stage at FailCon to talk about their mistakes and what they learnt from them.

At advertising agency Wieden+Kennedy, failure is seen as a critical part of what they do. Founder Dan Wieden always says 'Fail Harder', and in the Portland office (where the agency first started) there is a big board with those very words written on it.

Neil Christie, head of Wieden+Kennedy's London office says, 'You can either have a culture where you say to people, "Whatever you do, don't screw up", or you can have a culture where you say,

"We are going to push you to do things that you don't know whether you can do and that we don't know whether it's possible to be done at all. If we aim high, we will achieve more than we would have done if we'd settled for average".

'Fail Harder is intended to be an incentive to set the bar high and try and achieve as much as possible. If we set the bar really high, we will achieve more than we thought possible than if we settled for less. I think part of that comes from working with Nike, the founding client. Athletes constantly push themselves every time to do more than they thought they could do. It's all about pushing and pushing and pushing and failing. And the creative process is a bit like that as well. There is no finish line. There is no right answer. It's always about trying and trying and failing and trying again.'

Failure is not only encouraged; it is also built into people's performance appraisals. The agency has several questions they ask all staff at every performance review, one of which is about failure. 'We ask everyone, "What was your bravest and best failure this year?"', explains Christie. 'We recognise that and encourage people to try things that sometimes they can't do. If they're never failing, then the suggestion is that they're not trying hard enough.'

★★★

At the Tata Group, the idea of encouraging failure is taken to another level and is actually given a formal reward. The Tata Group is over 140 years old, comprises over 100 different companies, and has almost half a million employees globally—not the kind of company you would initially suspect to embrace risk-taking and failure.

Innovation is core to the Tata Group, and one of the ways it signals this is through its annual InnoVista Awards, which celebrate the most successful innovations Tata Group has launched. The InnoVista Awards regularly attract over two thousand entries from around the world. You are probably thinking—well, that's not particularly innovative or 'risky'—running an awards program for innovation. And indeed it is not. What *is* innovative is the awards *categories*.

InnoVista, like most innovation recognition programs, pays tribute to the Group's most outstanding and most promising innovations. But there is also a category called Dare to Try, which was launched back in 2009. This category is reserved for ideas that were attempted but that, according to the Tata Group website, 'have fallen short of achieving optimum results'.

The Tata Group openly publishes information about winners of the Dare to Try award for the public to read about. There is a story about Sukk, a jelly drink that was launched in the UK and has achieved moderate sales — however, the company believes that with launches in new regions, the product could start to hit its stride. There is also a story about a portable heart-monitoring device with seemingly huge benefits for the Indian market that, when launched, failed to gain a significant audience.

When I share what the Tata Group is doing with its innovation awards with my own clients, they are invariably impressed. I have seen many of them create their own versions of the Dare to Try award, given it is such an effective and tangible way of saying to employees 'We are okay with failure — and in fact, we will even reward the really big ones!'

★★★

Pfizer's innovation program is called Dare to Try. Vice President of Worldwide Innovation Wendy Mayer, says the reason behind the program name was entirely about encouraging risk-taking. The name was born back in 2013 when Mayer was working with the Specialty Care business unit. The business unit had an objective around encouraging people to take 'thoughtful risk'. 'Our work with them actually produced the initial version of our Dare to Try program', says Mayer.

'The challenge that we continually faced within Pfizer was that the commercial side of the business would always lead towards running pilots, rather than experimenting', explains Mayer. 'Pilots are problematic. They cost a lot of time and money to develop and they don't disaggregate the idea into the components that could potentially drive or hinder success. Usually, with pilots, you get a binary decision: "Yes, it worked" or "No, it didn't work". We decided to employ more of the experimentation model — something that we do all the time on the research

> ...it's not just about exposing ideas that were brilliant and worked ... it's also about learning from things that may not have worked as well.

side of the house—which is more about identifying some of the critical assumptions for success and doing quick, rapid experiments to either validate or disprove those assumptions. This enables us to do it quickly, to do it at a low cost, but also to pivot and change if some of those assumptions don't prove out. You don't have to destroy the whole idea.'

Through the Dare to Try program, Mayer says, they try to emphasise that it's not just about exposing ideas that were brilliant and worked, but that it's also about learning from things that may not have worked as well. 'It's more about daring to try', says Mayer. 'In some cases it will work, and in some cases it won't. With that, the name of the program has actually been a big component of its success, because it rings true to people with what we're trying to achieve across the organisation.'

One of the most famous examples of experimentation at Pfizer is Viagra. As is now innovation folklore, Viagra is a drug that was originally developed for treatment of angina—a condition that constricts the vessels that supply your heart with blood. The drug, originally known as UK-92480, was designed to relax the vessels to allow for better flow of blood to the heart. Unfortunately (or fortunately) the drug did not work as planned, but scientists in the lab began to notice an interesting little side effect—erections.

'Within our research organisation', says Mayer, 'the culture was always very much that the only way to succeed is to fail—as is generally the case in scientific research. You have to do a lot of experimentation and learn and then build on the learnings of that experimentation to ultimately achieve a success. Viagra was being developed as a cardiovascular medication, and part of learning from your failure is understanding what happened and doing an evaluation of the situation so that you can call out the learning and understand how to build off of those learnings.

'That culture enabled that new direction to be identified. The scientists found that it wasn't panning out as they had hoped as a cardiovascular medication, but in accepting the studies that had been done, and some of the feedback that was coming back from patients who were participating in the trials, it became evident that there was this other effect that could potentially present an opportunity. To me, it's a really good example of accepting failure and, very importantly, the value of learning from failure. We're trying to take more aspects of that culture and apply them now to our commercial organisation.'

★★★

One of the reasons taking risks is so scary is because the outcome of taking the risk is full of uncertainty. Wharton Management professor Jennifer Mueller and her colleagues were keen to investigate how the risk of uncertainty affects people's reactions to innovative pursuits. Mueller divided people into two groups. The first group was told that after the study, they would be eligible for an additional payment for participating, which would be decided at random — thus creating a small amount of uncertainty in that group. The second group, the control group, did not receive this information.

The two groups went on to evaluate a prototype for a new running shoe. The researchers found that, compared with the control group, those who had been primed to feel a small amount of uncertainty actually rated the prototype as being less viable. Instead, the uncertainty group preferred more practical solutions.

Interestingly, even people who rated high on open-mindedness weren't immune to this effect. When we are faced with uncertainty, we are motivated to reduce uncertainty. This results in negative associations with creativity, so that people instead prefer practical ideas where one can visualise the output, or familiar ideas (to make them feel safer), or ideas that reinforce the status quo.

One strategy for increasing people's propensity for, and comfort with, risk and ambiguity can be found in regulatory focus theory.

This theory suggests that individuals are likely to adopt one of two mindsets when pursuing goals: promotion-focused or prevention-focused.

- People who adopt a promotion focus (which has nothing to do with seeking a promotion at work, despite the label) are focused on their aspirations and long-term goals and exploring possibilities, and are all about maximising gains.

- People who adopt a prevention focus are more focused on minimising losses; they tend to have a shorter-term focus, and are concerned with fulfilling their immediate duties.

A promotion-focus mindset involves adopting what researchers call 'eagerness behaviours' (such as risk-taking activities) whereas a prevention focus involves engaging in more vigilant behaviours such as being cautious.

Research tells us that people's willingness to take risks is predictive of creative workplace behaviour such as the generation of useful and inventive suggestions. Regulatory focus theory predicts that individuals with a promotion-focused mindset are more likely to demonstrate creative and risk-taking behaviours. Promotion focus has also been shown to result in innovation-friendly behaviours in the workplace, including increased motivation to collaborate, feeling a sense of purpose, being open to feedback, and seeking new opportunities.

There are several strategies that you can use to put yourself in a promotion-focused state.

- Focus on your long-term aspirations rather than your immediate duties in the short term.

- Focus on finding what can be learned from failure rather than placing blame. When people are blamed for a mistake it fosters a prevention mindset and people will become even more focused on avoiding failure and mistakes.

- Use a promotion focus to frame challenges that require innovative thinking. For example, if you are trying to increase positive word-of-mouth, consider phrasing a challenge like 'How can we ensure that our customers are delighted time and time again?' as opposed to 'How can we reduce the number of disgruntled customers?'

★★★

One of the things that inevitably happens to companies as they grow is that the number and complexity of processes also grows. There is a good reason why this happens—growth brings with it chaos, and processes help to minimise the chaos so that things can run in an orderly fashion. However, what often ends up happening is that processes and bureaucracy get in the way of innovation. They make it very difficult for individuals and teams to take risks, because processes are designed to do the opposite: mitigate risk, minimise errors and prioritise efficiency over flexibility. And the flow-on effect is an increasingly prevention-focused mindset.

> ... 'Everything is in beta'. Nothing is set in stone and everything is eligible for change.

One solution to this problem is to move people into a promotion-focused mindset by seeing every process as having room for improvement. What this means in reality is that rather than viewing processes as inhibitors to an innovation culture, see every process as an opportunity for innovation.

At Inventium, we have a saying that 'Everything is in beta'. Nothing is set in stone and everything is eligible for change. When new employees start, I set up fortnightly meetings for their first six weeks. These meetings are critical for me, as they capture a person's thinking when they are still fresh to the organisation and everything we do — both externally and internally. As well as asking the new recruit how they are going and what they are enjoying, I also (and, I believe, more importantly) ask them the following questions:

- What are you finding most frustrating?

- What are you finding stupid?

- What has surprised you?

The answers to these questions are always illuminating. A few years ago I was in one of these catch-ups with a senior consultant who had recently started with Inventium. He made the observation that while the team seemed very close-knit, he was surprised that the consultants all worked in a very isolated fashion. No-one collaborated on projects and there was limited discussion about the work they were doing (other than in a weekly work-in-progress meeting). I had failed to notice this, but as soon as it was pointed out I could see exactly what he was talking about. I changed several structures within the company to ensure that from that point on collaboration was a regular occurrence. And now, several years later, it is rare to find a project at Inventium where there is no collaboration between consultants.

One of the best things about saying 'Everything is in beta' is that the team at Inventium is always suggesting ways to improve how we work. Early in 2015 we launched The Odd One Out, Melbourne's first workshop venue designed along lines scientifically proven to increase creative thought. We had seen a gap in the market for a brilliant space for off-sites, innovation workshops and other corporate events and decided to create a space ourselves.

When we first set up the space, anyone wanting to book The Odd One Out had to email through an enquiry, and our venue manager would then respond. We would then have to check the calendar to see if the date was available and have a few back-and-forth conversations with the client. Many steps later, the date would be locked in. After going through this process a few times, our venue manager took it upon himself to see if he could automate it.

A few hours later, after playing around with The Odd One Out's website a booking function had been created. Potential clients can view the venue's calendar and see if a specific date is free, agree to the terms and conditions of booking the venue and then, without having to say even one word to us, lock in their booking for The Odd One Out.

★★★

When we recruit for any new role at Inventium, we are always on the lookout for people with a learning orientation. These are people who are always seeking to learn — even if it compromises performance. This might sound slightly strange — surely we would be looking for people who are 'performers' and are all about the outcome. But what we know from research is that those with a learning orientation:

- are more likely to respond positively to constructive feedback

- consistently seek to improve and develop (and so tend to be stronger contributors to an organisation and innovation)

- are significantly more comfortable with failure

- consistently exhibit higher creativity at work.

People with a learning orientation are more likely to be motivated by the desire to develop themselves through the acquisition and mastery of new skills. They derive satisfaction out of doing so. In work environments, these people have the motivation to persist with complex issues that require hard work and initiative; and they also enjoy learning the new skills and techniques required to complete these challenging tasks. This tendency increases the development of creativity, as motivation and knowledge are key drivers of creative potential.

At finance and accounting software firm Intuit (much like some of the companies mentioned earlier in this chapter) experimentation and learning are a big part of the culture — and the only bad experiment is one you don't learn anything from. Vice President of Intuit Labs Incubator Hugh Molotsi, explains, 'We think of experiments as learning vehicles. That we're trying ultimately to learn how to build great solutions for customers. Experiments give us insights into what that ultimate solution should be'.

In addition to simply running experiments, pace is considered critical. 'If you spend three days building something and then experimenting on it and then learning from it', says Molotsi, 'that's a great outcome. But if you spend three months building something and running an experiment and it's a failure in that you didn't build something that customers responded to positively, then the missed opportunity is that you spent three months on it when you could have done other things in that time. It's really about the pace of innovation — how quickly you can build your minimum viable products and test them, then get those insights and that learning'.

Once a month, at Intuit's innovation centre in Mountain View, California, the company runs Incubation Week. Anyone in the company is allowed to participate. Typically, five to ten teams (with between two and seven people per team) will sign up for any given Innovation Week. Teams are given pre-work to ensure they arrive on the Monday with an idea that will provide value to customers' lives. That way, they are able to start building their idea on the Monday with the aim of releasing it by the Friday.

'Teams arrive on a Monday with their idea', explains Molotsi. 'And by Friday, they've got an MVP [minimum viable product] that they're releasing to customers to test. It's a one-week turnaround to build an MVP. Leaders see it as a very modest investment of people's time in terms of getting the MVP out. It really takes the pressure off when you can turn things around quickly.'

★★★

One of the biggest killers of innovation and risk-taking is a blame culture. The strongest characteristic of a blame culture is that fingers get pointed when something goes wrong. And if people are worried about being blamed (because this is what happens when something goes wrong), people will stop taking risks and play it safe—because if they play it safe, nothing will go wrong. At least in theory.

> One of the biggest killers of innovation and risk-taking is a blame culture. The strongest characteristic of a blame culture is that fingers get pointed when something goes wrong.

Several years ago Etsy introduced 'blameless post-mortems' to help ensure they avoided going down the path of blame. 'When things go wrong at Etsy', explains CEO Chad Dickerson, 'we get everyone into a room a day or so after the problem occurs. We go through a timeline and then we create a list of what we call remediation items, and these are things that we need to do better next time. We force ourselves to actually fix the systems that need to be fixed'.

In contrast, imagine a blame culture and what happens there. Etsy CTO John Allspaw, wrote a post on Etsy's blog, 'Code as Craft', about what happens when a culture of blame is rife. Allspaw describes the following cycle for blaming and shaming:

1  *Engineer takes action and contributes to a failure or incident.*

2  *Engineer is punished, shamed, blamed, or retrained.*

3  *Reduced trust between engineers on the ground (the 'sharp end') and management (the 'blunt end') looking for someone to scapegoat.*

4  *Engineers become silent on details about actions/situations/ observations, resulting in 'Cover-Your-Ass' engineering (from fear of punishment).*

5  *Management becomes less aware and informed on how work is being performed day to day, and engineers become less educated on lurking or latent conditions for failure due to silence mentioned in #4, above.*

Risk-taking

6   *Errors more likely, latent conditions can't be identified due to #5, above.*

7   *Repeat from step 1.*

*We need to avoid this cycle. We want the engineer who has made an error [to] give details about why (either explicitly or implicitly) he or she did what they did; why the action made sense to them at the time. This is paramount to understanding the pathology of the failure. The action made sense to the person at the time they took it, because if it hadn't made sense to them at the time, they **wouldn't have taken the action in the first place.***

'We take problems seriously', Dickerson says. 'But when you don't think you're going to get yelled at for making a mistake, I think people actually make fewer mistakes. You're also more willing to take risks because you're not going to get in trouble.'

There have been many incidents and problems examined by blameless post-mortem at Etsy. These have ranged from the time a developer managed to break the function that lets users 'favourite' or bookmark an item, through to an issue with seating arrangements during a new office expansion.

There are three basic principles of running a blameless post-mortem:

1   *Assume that people are operating from a place of good will.*
    No-one comes to work to do a bad job. When accidents happen it is almost never because someone intended for it to go wrong. Rather, mistakes happen as a natural result of working with complex systems. Not all mistakes have catastrophic consequences (the majority of them don't) and success depends on making mistakes. The key is to make an effort to understand how people viewed their work as they were doing it. This requires supporting the people who have made mistakes, and encouraging them to 'teach' everyone about it.

2   *Identify conditions, not culprits.* 'We have a ground rule that
    the purpose of a post-mortem is to find out what happened
    and how to make it better, not to find a person to blame',
    Dickerson told Business Insider Australia. 'As a result, what
    we've seen is a company that's learning and moving faster.'
    Therefore, the goal is to find out how the mistake happened,
    and to understand how to change things to prevent (as much
    as is possible) similar mistakes happening in the future.

3   *Don't rush it.* Blameless post-mortems at Etsy are always held
    at least 24 hours after the mistake or failure happened. This
    gives time for emotions to die down (emotions tend to be
    very high just after the event). In addition, people can take
    time to own up to their mistakes even when provided with a
    forum to do so.

★★★

One other example of a company that has completely embraced
risk-taking and the constant possibility of failure as part of daily
life is Buzz Products. If you've travelled on an international
flight recently, chances are your amenities pack was created by
Buzz Products. Buzz is an international product design agency
specialising in the travel industry. A few years ago, they caught
wind of the fact that Qantas was rethinking its entire check-in
process. Rather than wait for an invitation to pitch for the project,
Buzz assembled a cross-functional group of leaders who set about
working on a solution to make the check-in process seamless
for customers.

Barry Gold, managing director of Buzz Products, recalls pulling
together an A-class team. 'We had the agency's design director,
our head of supply chain, our creative director and a couple of
others. There was no clear brief at that time because there were so
many moving parts and so many other companies involved. There
were people working on the terminal, the infrastructure in the
terminal, the software platforms, and so on. It was risky because

we had no brief and no guarantee that anything would come of it. But cheekily, we started working with the other companies that had already been contracted, and from there we started building a brief for ourselves.

'We have a saying at Buzz which is 'run it like you've won it'. And that's exactly what we did with Qantas. I think many companies would have played it more carefully and more professionally than we did, but it worked. The outcome was the Q-Bag Tag. It was a world-first integration of radio-frequency identification technology into a bag tag that allows passengers' travel details to be synchronised with their baggage.

While in retrospect these things can sometimes seem smooth sailing, that certainly wasn't the case for this project. One of the biggest setbacks with the Q-Bag Tag project happened right at the end of the journey when Qantas brought in an external procurement company to try to cut costs. 'These guys came in and said to us that we needed to halve our price. That was pretty much the whole conversation. It's always disheartening to get to a point like that. But we simply said no. The thing was, because of the approach and the risk-taking, and because we'd got so far, there was just no choice for them. Not taking us on at our asking price would have meant there was no way Qantas would meet its deadlines. In the end, Buzz was able to deliver a world-first product, within an incredibly tight timeline, and Qantas was so happy.

'There were so many crises like that along the way', recalls Gold. 'That's true of almost every project, every interesting project. But it's all about how the team responds to these crises. It comes down to humour and openness and being able to fail.'

# KEY POINTS

- Having a culture where risk-taking is tolerated, and indeed encouraged, is critical for building an innovation culture.

- Think about initiatives and actions that you can put in place to illustrate that your company doesn't just pay lip-service to risk-taking, but actually does it.

- Consider having a company award for innovations that were not commercial successes (and were actually failures), but where the learnings were really rich.

- Reframe risk-taking in a positive way, such as talking about how risks provide people with the opportunity to learn.

- Consider setting performance measures around people's risk-taking to show you are serious about wanting employees to take risks in the pursuit of innovation.

- Holding blameless post-mortems can be an effective process for avoiding (or overcoming) a blame culture and instead keeping the focus on identifying 'conditions, not culprits'.

- By treating everything as being in beta, you allow and empower others to constantly be thinking about how things can be improved.

# CHAPTER 12

# COHESION

## We're all in this together

Of all the variables Samuel Hunter and his colleagues identified in their meta-analysis, the number one driver of innovation culture is one that academics refer to as 'positive interpersonal exchange'. What this translates to in practice is an organisation where all employees feel a sense of togetherness — as if they are all working as one big team towards a larger goal. There is minimal conflict (except for the healthy type of debate discussed in chapter 4), and people work together harmoniously. Of all the variables that Hunter and his team explored, this one is arguably the hardest to achieve. It is not something that any one individual can change on his or her own, unlike many of the other variables discussed in this book. It is something that needs to be led from the top, but also driven from the bottom.

In a review of several meta-analyses Silvia da Costa, from the University of the Basque Country, and several of her colleagues looked at the impact of cohesion across employees within an organisation. The researchers found that when cohesion is high, 65 per cent of people will demonstrate above-average creativity and innovation in their performance. In contrast, only 32 per cent of people working in organisations with low levels of cohesion will show above-average innovativeness.

Innovation programs, when executed well, can be great unifiers and drivers of cohesion. They allow everyone to have a voice and unite people in solving the organisation's biggest and smallest challenges. When Innov8, Coca-Cola Amatil's innovation program, was rolled out across the region, one of the most striking and unexpected benefits of the program was its effect on employees' levels of engagement.

Derek O'Donnell, the creator of Innov8, recalls the impact of the program. 'One of our offices had suffered from very low engagement scores which were in the mid 30s. In the three years after we launched Innov8 in this office, our employee engagement scores skyrocketed to the mid 70s. And more importantly, the office maintained those scores. Since the launch of Innov8, this office has produced some of the strongest leadership in innovation. They look at it from the perspective of "We're going to celebrate people. No matter what their position. No matter what their level is. We're going to show respect for them. We want to make sure they feel their voices are heard". The positivity that builds off that is remarkable.'

O'Donnell made a distinctive choice early on about which innovations would be progressed and which would be left behind. The number one criteria he encouraged leaders to look for was the passion of the idea's creator. 'We refused to bring an innovation through unless the owner wanted to come with it. We had some attractive ideas brought to the table that we didn't act on. And we didn't act on them because the person that brought it forward wasn't willing to show their own passion to act on it.

'I myself rejected some exciting ideas that would have delivered benefits to the business because the person didn't show passion behind their idea. They wanted to give it to somebody else to take over. I said, "Well, if you can't show the passion, you can't ask anybody else to". And people always challenge me on that but I knew in the long term it was the right decision, providing an opportunity for constructive feedback and coaching to help the person get behind their idea and bring it to life.'

★★★

In technology circles, people talk about 'setting the default to open'. This relates to concepts such as creating open source technology (where the source code is released for other developers to use and change) through to 'open information'. With 'open information', companies use data they have on customers in a way that will provide value back to the customer and also give customers control over the data. And the concept of openness is incredibly important in helping to create a cohesive environment and driving a culture where innovation flourishes.

One of the biggest points that comes up when I speak to leaders at highly innovative companies is that they share very openly. Given that senior leader support is so critical for innovation performance, leadership that displays openness and transparency has been shown to encourage innovative behaviour. This can be demonstrated in many ways.

When I asked Chad Dickerson, CEO of Etsy, what his favourite innovation at Etsy had been, one that immediately sprang to his mind was the Etsy API (application program interface — a set of routines, protocols and tools that provides the building blocks for programmers to build software that can sit within an existing program or website). 'We've built an API and basically everything you do on Etsy, like listing items and displaying items, you can do on your API. What the API does is it allows anyone to build anything—internally or externally. One of the most significant things that the API produced was an iPhone app. Up until November 2011, Etsy didn't have an iPhone app, which was something that we really needed to do. A developer who didn't work for Etsy had built an Etsy iPhone app using our API and we basically called him up and said, "Do you want to work for Etsy?" We bought his app, he became an employee of Etsy, and over the course of about six weeks, we cleaned it up.

'From the time we called him to the time we had the Etsy app in the app store was basically six or eight weeks. Not only did we get the core of our iPhone app, we got a developer who, on his own with no relationship to Etsy initially, was motivated enough to build something for Etsy and then we hired him.' To date, and perhaps not at all surprisingly, he has been an excellent employee.

'API is probably my favourite idea because it's like having the whole world as your R&D team.' And of course, none of this would have happened if Dickerson had chosen for Etsy to *not* operate in such an open way through releasing the API.

At Inventium, one of our core values is Share Generously. This value arose from a conversation I had with another innovation consultant, a man named Ken Wall, in my first year of running Inventium.

I had just come from a meeting with Inventium's lawyer, who was on my back to trademark or copyright everything, given that as a consultancy our intellectual property was our biggest asset. I was telling Ken about this meeting and Ken stopped me and said, 'Amantha, you have a fundamental choice to make. You can come at business from a mindset of scarcity and act as if there is not enough work out there for everyone. If you make this choice, you will need to hold your cards close to your chest, protect your IP ferociously, and not share it with anyone except if they are paying you for it.

'The other way you could approach business is from a mindset of plenty. You can act with the assumption that there is more than enough work out there for everyone and that there are plenty of fish in the sea. If you make this choice, it will allow you to not worry so much about protecting your IP, but instead, get it out there as widely as possible.'

This conversation stuck with me and even now, eight years on from it, I remember it vividly. It fundamentally shaped my beliefs around how I wanted to run Inventium and, as a result, one of our core values became Share Generously. Having clear values makes it easier to make decisions, so when someone on my team is given the choice of whether to share or not to share, they will always default to sharing. This might be in the form of someone seeing us deliver a keynote and asking for a copy of our slides (we always say yes); it might be in the form of a client wanting more detailed training notes from a session we delivered (we always say yes); or it might be in the form of sharing a great deal of our IP through our weekly e-newsletters (we share a lot).

Another initiative we started a few years ago was called Pay What You Want innovation training for the not-for-profit sector. The majority of Inventium's clients are large corporates but we are all passionate about doing more work with the not-for-profit sector. We borrowed an idea from Melbourne's Lentil As Anything restaurant, where diners are simply asked to 'pay what they would like' for their meal. We ask participants to pay what they want, which has resulted in poetry, unusual sculptures, and food (which is definitely our favourite way of being paid!).

★★★

Research has shown that when people are united by a common vision or purpose—one that they actually believe in—organisation-wide cohesion will be significantly higher. At advertising agency Wieden+Kennedy, people are united through a very clear purpose. 'When anybody joins this place', explains Neil Christie, who heads up the London office, 'there is one thing that we always say. The founding principle of the agency is to help people do the best work of their lives. Everybody knows that's what the place is for and that's what we do. People will call you out on it as well, if there are things that are getting in the way of that'.

While Christie admits that staying true to that on every job and on every client is tough, it is the principle that guides all behaviour. 'What we have to try and do is create the environment in which that's possible. I've actually just come out of a meeting now where we're talking about it, saying, "Do we think we can do the best work of our lives on this job? If not, we shouldn't do it".'

CEO Brad Smith describes Intuit's mission as 'To improve our customers' financial lives so profoundly, they could never imagine going back to the old way of doing things'. Hugh Molotsi, vice president of Intuit Labs Incubator, explains that the solutions people come up with for customers are really about making their lives better. 'The notion of purpose is that you're doing something that is bigger than yourself, it's bigger than your self-interests or your company's self-interests. You're really trying to make this positive impact on the world.'

At the Australian arm of global pharmaceutical company AbbVie, Managing Director Kirsten O'Doherty says that the organisation is united by its genuine desire to improve patients' lives. 'Our vision is that we will innovate and collaborate to create a remarkable impact for patients. It's not just a slogan that's put up, because that would be easy. We recently had a few new people start and they all spontaneously said that the thing they've noticed almost immediately is that the vision is real, not just lip-service. It's really making a difference to patients and everyone's role is unique and individual in contributing to that.'

One of the ways in which this translates is in how the company talks about and emphasises sales and growth. 'We just had our national conference', says O'Doherty. 'And instead of saying, "Here's our sales results and here's the growth", we talk about how many patients are being treated, how many more patients are due to be treated, and how many more patients we expect to have treated next year. They're really important metrics.'

And the sales team, who might have come from traditional sales-focused cultures in other organisations, are encouraged to focus on total measures of impact instead. 'I'll say to the sales team very clearly, many times, because some of them have come from other companies —"It doesn't only matter what our sales results are. At AbbVie, you'll be measured on patient access to treatment and the number of patients we have treated".'

As well as keeping patients front and centre of the company vision and goals, patients are regularly invited to come into AbbVie's Australian head office in Sydney to share their story. 'We had a patient recently who's in one of our clinical trials for medication that treats some types of chronic lymphocytic leukaemia. This patient had her daughter with her and she went through her whole history: her diagnosis, the other treatment she'd had, finally getting on the clinical trial, and the result she's had. These opportunities to hear patient stories are not only moving but also incredibly motivating. I think just about everybody in the room was in tears.'

★★★

The natural partner to a purpose or vision is a set of values that sit underneath. At many organisations, company values are ridiculed, ignored or seen as irrelevant. But when they are done well they can be an extremely effective way to get everyone feeling as though they are playing for the same team. International product design agency Buzz Products is a unique beast in that the company has managed to articulate three core values that are known, respected and embraced by every single employee.

The first of the three values is 'Follow the yellow brick road'. 'That's all around the story of the *Wizard of Oz*', explains Managing Director Barry Gold, 'and how there were the four characters who were all incredibly different but worked together to achieve a goal'.

The second of the values is 'Go where the wild things are', an homage to the 1963 children's book by Maurice Sendak, a story of a brave young boy named Max who, after being sent to his room without supper, goes sailing out to sea to where the wild things are. After taming the beasts he is crowned king of the wild things and romps around with the creatures, and then he returns home to bed (and a hot supper). 'That value is all about risk-taking', explains Gold.

The final value is 'Buzz twist and lime'. 'We've got this phrase at Buzz, "Have you given it the Buzz twist?". That's common lingo around here, which is about putting a unique, Buzz-like angle to every innovation we produce. The 'lime' refers to bringing the Buzz twist to life. It's not just an idea that you came up with in a meeting. It's about making it real.'

In addition to the values, Buzz introduced Buddy Groups to help build strong ties and a sense of cohesion across the organisation. Each Buddy Group consists of four or five people who work in separate teams, and when a new person joins Buzz they are immediately allocated to a Buddy Group. Each Buddy Group is given a nominal budget of around $15 per person per month. Gold explains, 'Groups might go bowling, or check out a new café, or go to a museum. They are allowed to do whatever they want, as long as it's together. It really strengthens the relationships across the company. And when there's someone new coming in, it's a really great way to be inducted and feel at home'.

And it's not just the Buddy Group that makes newcomers feel part of the team. Whenever a new person starts, everyone else in the 100-person business wears a name-tag—a nice but simple touch that makes newcomers feel immediately welcomed and included.

# KEY POINTS

- Organisation-wide cohesion and the feeling that everyone is playing for the same team is the most impactful driver of an innovation culture.

- Innovation programs in and of themselves can act as a great unifier, encouraging everyone to band together to solve a set of challenges and opportunities.

- Sharing generously and being open are important traits in driving cohesion and innovation.

- Having a strong and meaningful purpose can be effective at bringing people together and making them feel that they are on the same team.

- Consider creating cross-departmental Buddy Groups to create connections across the organisation where there might otherwise have been none.

# CHAPTER 13

# PARTICIPATION

## The workplace isn't Hollywood—why we don't need stars

If you have done any reading about innovation, you have probably heard of hack days, or hackathons. The concept has gained popularity in the last few years, and is now a staple event at many tech companies. The hack day concept actually started at Yahoo back in 2005, when Chad Dickerson (now CEO of Etsy) was working in the Search division.

'One of the things I noticed when I was at Yahoo was a website inside Yahoo called the Idea Factory', explains Dickerson. 'The idea behind the Idea Factory was to have a suggestion box for ideas. If you worked at Yahoo and you thought you had the solution to world peace, you could go to the Idea Factory and say, "If the world just worked this way then this would happen".'

Dickerson noticed that the Idea Factory was never short of ideas. Indeed, everyone in the company had lots of ideas but unfortunately, ideas don't really mean anything unless they are implemented. When Dickerson started Hack Day at Yahoo, it was with the idea that a team of people could take an idea and, within a compressed period of time, actually build it into something tangible.

A critical factor of Dickerson's hack days was that people were given free rein. 'Inside a corporation that's difficult, because a corporation has its objectives and you're actually paying people, but I had really great support from the management at Yahoo', says Dickerson. 'I came up with the concept through hearing about what was happening with start-ups of five or eight people. I wanted to see if you could do it with 3000 people.

'We basically set a 24-hour period and got management buy-in to allow the engineers to do whatever they wanted for that day. The only rules were: take 24 hours; come up with something; build a prototype; and present it at the end of the day. There were no assigned teams and no assigned workspaces.

'The premise of Hack Day was that developers had great ideas and they could execute them. If you didn't tell them what to do, they would do amazing things. And that's exactly what happened.'

Dickerson's Search division at Yahoo had 3000 people, and several hundred participated in the first Hack Day. 'I didn't even ask people to sign up, I just said, "Today's the day for people to do whatever they want and we're going to have a sheet for you to sign up to present your demo at the end of the day". At the end of the day I didn't know who had built what, as there was really no central authority. We had 70 teams and they each had something to show.'

Yahoo ended up running Hack Days in the United States, the UK and Asia. 'People just did creative work', Dickerson recalls. 'And the theory that I had was actually proven — that if you have smart people and give them room, they'll do amazing things. It was proven over and over again. The only thing different, really, in the different places was the food the people ate. We had samosas in Bangalore, and we had pizza in California.'

When Dickerson moved to Etsy he took the concept of hack days a step further and created Hack Week. During this week, literally the entire company is invited to stop working on 'business as usual' and to build prototypes, with the aim of having production-ready code at the end of the week. Instead of receiving a prize for the best prototype, the reward is actually pushing the changes out to the site.

One of the winning teams from an Etsy Hack Week built a system where users would be able to 'favourite' an item that appeared in search results, rather than having to click on the item first. It was a very small idea that had a big impact—after the idea was implemented, 'favouriting' activity went up by 30 per cent.

Reflecting on what hack days and hack weeks do for an organisation's culture, Dickerson says, 'Having hack weeks implicitly says, "I trust the team". It says "I know that when I give you freedom you're going to do great work". That's a really powerful dynamic because, in my mind, companies that don't do things like that, or say "We could never do that", are saying they don't trust their employees. When you have trusted employees and the employees trust you, they do better work, they're happy, and they do more innovative work.'

★★★

One of the most effective ways to encourage participation in innovation is to have a clear innovation process. While the focus of this book is on innovation culture, I will deviate for a moment to explain what a good innovation process looks like. There are several clear steps:

1  create an innovation mission

2  scan your environment (and ask customers what frustrates them)

3  set the challenge you need to solve

4  generate ideas

5  shortlist your ideas

6  experiment

7  scale

8  promote.

As mentioned in chapter 10, a best-practice innovation process does not start with idea generation—despite the fact that this is how many companies operate. Instead, the process needs to begin with clear innovation missions, which provide strategic focus areas for innovation. For example, an innovation mission might be 'Becoming carbon neutral by 2020', 'Creating the next big thing in Category X' or 'Helping small businesses to use the internet safely'.

★★★

Once these clear goals are set, the process should then progress into the Scan stage. The Scan stage is all about the customer. It is during this stage that you need to encourage people to get out of the building and speak to real customers. Many organisations fall into the trap of simply asking customers what they want, or what is important to them. However, we know that customers' ideas can be unreliable. People are not very good at predicting what they might want or need in the future. As Henry Ford is reputed to have said, 'If I had asked people what they wanted, they would have said faster horses'.

During the Scan stage, rather than asking customers what they want, ask them what frustrates them. At Inventium, we refer to this as our Peeve Points process—asking questions of customers in order to understand their biggest peeves. To properly uncover a peeve point, one of the things you can do is ask a customer to talk you through how they currently approach the particular activity or process you are interested in improving, whether that be washing the dishes, consuming music, posting a package or cleaning the barbecue. Ask them about every step in the process. Washing dishes, for example, starts with creating the dirty dishes in the first place; then possibly stacking them in an interim area (such as beside the sink); then finding time to load them into the dishwasher (possibly doing this as one big task, or doing this in dribs and drabs); then programming the dishwasher on the most appropriate wash cycle; then waiting for the dishwasher to run its cycle; and then, finally, unloading the dishwasher.

When you are asking customers about every step in the process, look for points of frustration or workarounds. For example, when Inventium was working with a client to innovate the area of barbecue cleaning, we found that one of the biggest workarounds (consumers creating their own solution in the absence of the market providing them with an adequate one) was using a scrunched-up newspaper to clean the surface of the barbecue. As you zone in on these workarounds or points of frustration, ask the customer how satisfied they are with the current solution to their problem. And if there is a gap between their frustration and today's available solutions, you have uncovered a great opportunity for innovation.

★★★

The third step of an effective innovation process involves setting the specific challenge that you will aim to solve. This should spring directly from the biggest frustration or unmet need you uncovered during the Scan stage. Make sure your challenge is clear and specific, but also take the opportunity to make it exciting too. For example, don't ask 'How can we improve market share for product X among school-aged children?' Instead, ask 'How can we create the next schoolyard craze via product X?' Boring challenges beget boring ideas. Exciting challenges lead to exciting ideas.

After you have set your challenge, move on to generating ideas for solving the challenge. (Yes, idea generation is actually the fourth step in a best-practice innovation process, *not* the first!)

★★★

After generating ideas, start to make decisions about which ideas to progress and which to leave behind. One piece of advice around making good decisions comes from the study of decision fatigue. What we know about every human brain is that it has limited capacity to make good decisions. Every morning, when we wake up, our decision-making resources are replenished. However, over the course of the day, our resources get depleted with every single decision we make — and decision fatigue sets in. Essentially, the later in the day you make a decision, the worse the quality of that decision will be.

Decision fatigue leads to us taking the path of least resistance — essentially, making the easiest, least risky decision. In the case of innovation, you simply can't afford to let this happen. Make your big decisions first thing in the morning.

Once you've decided which concepts to take through, be sure to avoid the big mistakes companies tend to make at this stage of the innovation process: moving next to a) focus group testing or b) creating a business case.

Let's focus first on the problems with focus groups. In my previous working life, when I was a consumer psychologist within advertising agencies, I ran literally hundreds of focus groups. If you have never watched or participated in a focus group, it is basically a group of eight or so customers who are asked a series of questions about a particular product. The aim is to get a good sense of how they feel about the product and, in the case of concept testing for innovation, to understand whether they would purchase the product.

There are two main problems with focus groups. First, people, in general, are nice. They want to be liked and they don't want to offend other people. So as a focus group moderator, you generally hear views through a rose-coloured lens. Second — and this is the biggest problem with focus groups — people are really bad at predicting what they will do or how they will act in the future. While they might genuinely think your product is great and say they would definitely buy it, research suggests that intentions rarely match behaviour. Once we have a concept to test, we need to make sure we are measuring behaviour rather than intentions.

Let's now look at the second big mistake companies make — going straight to business case. In a way, this is even worse that doing focus group testing — at least focus group testing involves the customer! Instead, a business case involves making many assumptions about the customer (without ever talking to one) and building lots of fancy spreadsheets that have lines increasing from left to right, to build a really compelling case for the concept they are trying to 'sell' to management. I have never read a business case that didn't stack up —but I have certainly seen a lot of cases where what happened in real life was completely different from what was described in the business case.

When it comes to breakthrough or disruptive innovation, business cases are problematic because they make assumptions without actually testing them with the end user. So, to help reduce failure rates, once you've decided which ideas to progress you need to go out and actually test those assumptions with real customers.

★★★

Once you have shortlisted concepts, the next stage of the innovation process is the experimentation stage. This is where you apply scientific methodology to actually test all your assumptions and iterate (that is, change and improve) your innovation according to what you find.

All good experiments start with setting hypotheses. In *The Lean Start Up*, Eric Ries talks about setting two types of hypotheses. Value hypotheses relate to your assumptions about why you think your customer will find the product valuable or useful and ultimately part with money (or something else of value) in exchange for the product. Growth hypotheses relate to your assumptions about how you think your product will grow its customer base.

Once you have generated a list of hypotheses, Ries suggests prioritising them from most risky to least risky. Test your riskiest hypotheses first. After working out which hypothesis you are going to test first, the next step is to create a minimum viable product. This is a stripped-down version of your product that allows you to learn and test your hypotheses.

The next step is to design an experiment that will demonstrate cause and effect—you might want to set up a control group and an experimental group, or conduct A/B testing—so you can draw conclusions about what behaviour change the product caused (if any). And after reviewing the results of your experiment to see whether or not your hypothesis was supported, you can make the decision about whether you need to change or iterate the product based on customer behaviour.

★★★

After running a series of experiments and refining and iterating your idea, you are ready to scale. This is generally the 'easy' part for organisations, given most are set up to implement projects on a daily basis!

Finally, having achieved all this, don't forget to promote what you have done — both internally and externally. You might feel this goes without saying, but I have encountered many organisations that fail to do a good job of this, particularly with regard to internal promotion (that is, sharing the story with employees). An example of this occurred when I was running an innovation training session with the business product development team of a large bank. The day before the training session, the bank had launched a revolutionary new technology product, so I was quite excited to ask the team about it and how it came to be. When I asked them about it, they frustratedly said that the first they had heard about it was when they read about it in the newspaper yesterday. Clearly this is not ideal.

★★★

Implementing an innovation process like the one I've described, and ensuring everyone in your organisation knows how to contribute to it, will make sure that there is a clear avenue for people to participate in innovation. Having an innovation process that sits outside the hierarchy of your organisation and encourages people to contribute to it (whether by identifying customer challenges to solve or generating solutions to challenges, for example), is an important ingredient in having a culture where innovation thrives.

A question that I am often asked is whether innovation should be compartmentalised or democratised. That is, should innovation be everybody's job or just the job of a select group of people? Professor Annick Castiaux from the Louvain School of Management set out with one of her colleagues to investigate that exact question: If everyone is encouraged to contribute to innovation, will that mean that no-one actually contributes because accountability is diluted across the organisation? The researchers interviewed a group of R&D managers and quality managers from several different industries, asking about their approaches to innovation and how employees were (or were not) encouraged to innovate. They also reviewed several companies' approaches to encouraging employees to participate in innovation, and the outcomes.

Castiaux found that having an environment where every employee was encouraged to participate in innovation was beneficial for innovation, specifically when employees were encouraged to generate ideas and solutions for specific issues. At Renault, for example, the management team would decide on several challenges that were important to solve and put these out to the entire organisation. Between 1999 and 2006, the percentage of employees involved in solving problems grew from 15 per cent to 75 per cent. Renault had estimated that by 2006 the financial gain from having so many employees participate in the program was around €45 million.

Some organisations have taken the approach that innovation should be compartmentalised and left only to a few star performers. One such organisation is Yahoo. For several years Yahoo operated Brickhouse — a separate division that was designed to be an idea incubator. It was a start-up environment but with all the resources that a large multinational organisation is able to provide. Brickhouse was created to lead the development of new and breakthrough ideas for the company, with the theory being that the main body of Yahoo was not set up to support breakthrough innovations and had squashed this type of thinking in the past.

'The way I'd describe it is more a start-up incubator inside Yahoo', explains Chad Dickerson, who used to

*(continued)*

head up Brickhouse before moving on to join Etsy. 'We worked in small teams, the size of most start-ups, of three to five people, and we answered the question of "How do we build products that could become big businesses?"

I think it was a noble effort but what I learned from that—and this is actually one of the reasons I came to Etsy, because Etsy was quite small at the time—is that it's very hard to do start-ups inside a large company. Because you still have all the challenges of being part of a larger company, everything from payroll systems to procurement systems.

'If you needed a server in Yahoo, even if you were working for Brickhouse, there's one purchasing process and you had to wait just as long as the other guys. Whereas at Etsy—I'll never forget this. We needed a server during a holiday rush in my first year and I think I ordered one on my Amex and drove to the FedEx facility and picked it up and drove it to the data centre, all in the space of 48 hours.

'One of the biggest lessons I learned, because I lived through it, is that you can't compartmentalise innovation', says Dickerson. 'To me it's a warning sign that something is wrong or broken with the organisation.'

Sadly, but perhaps not surprisingly, Yahoo Brickhouse ended up closing two years after it opened.

One thing to note about democratising innovation is that it is far more effective to do this at the front end of innovation—the part where challenges are identified and problems are solved. Better to have the whole organisation working on identifying customer needs and frustrations and coming up with new and creative ways to solve these problems, rather than just a few people.

It's different at the back end of innovation—where the rubber hits the road and ideas start to be prototyped and implemented. This is where you actually do need to compartmentalise innovation and assign project teams to ideas. (Because otherwise, nothing will actually get done.)

★★★

Participation is one of the main cornerstones of Google's culture — represented through the idea of 'voice'. In *Work Rules!* Laszlo Bock describes what this means.

> *Voice means giving employees a real say in how the company is run. Either you believe people are good and you welcome their input, or you don't. For many organisations this is terrifying, but it is the only way to live in adherence to your values.*

One example of how Google encourages people to have a voice is a program called Bureaucracy Busters, launched by former CFO Patrick Pichette. Bureaucracy Busters is an annual program that asks Googlers to submit solutions to their biggest frustrations. Other Googlers are then able to vote on which ideas they want to see implemented. In the first year the program was run, 570 ideas were submitted and these ideas received over 55 000 votes between them. In general, the frustrations had come from relatively small issues that were easy to fix.

While this may seem like a straightforward solution to improving productivity, it is worth reflecting on how this type of situation is approached in your average organisation. Frustrations around bureaucracy and red tape are almost treated as a given — and accepted, albeit begrudgingly, by employees. Indeed, one of the most common barriers I hear our clients raise when it comes to innovation is that the amount of bureaucracy makes it impossible to do anything.

★★★

Another way to think about participation in the context of innovation is to see employees as not just idea generators, but as idea testers, too. At video-sharing site Vimeo, ideas are tested with employees before any changes are shipped to the public.

When Vimeo did an entire redesign of its site several years ago, they had staff using the new site internally for a few months instead of pushing the huge changes out to the public immediately. Dae Mellencamp, president of Vimeo, describes what these few months were like. 'It wasn't there. We knew it just wasn't but we couldn't figure out why. Over time, more people got involved figuring out little details and continually iterating and improving the site. Then finally, after several months of testing and iterating, we knew it was there. And we knew it was there because everybody was saying, "I don't want to go back to the old design. Don't make me go back to the old design".'

At Commonwealth Bank of Australia, providing employees with the chance to participate in the innovation process as idea testers has been rapidly and enthusiastically adopted in an initiative called Friends of the Lab. 'The purpose of Friends of the Lab,' explains Tiziana Bianco, Head of Innovation Lab at Commonwealth Bank of Australia, 'is to harness the passion and enthusiasm of the bank's employees and match this community with the need internally to test new products and concepts. We know that our employee base is largely representative of the Australian population so testing our concepts internally was not only seen as a great way to get feedback but also involve more employees in our innovation journey.'

Within six weeks of the program launching, 700 employees had signed up. 'The Friends of the Lab love being involved in early stage concept testing,' describes Bianco. 'For them, it's like being part of an internal Kickstarter campaign.' In return for their time and participation, the Friends of the Lab community receive exclusive invitations to events and innovation training sessions.

In addition to considering how employees can be encouraged to participate more in innovation, the Bank has also started to rethink the way it invites participation from its suppliers. A recent example involved the Bank embarking on the journey of transforming its Intranet, and wanted to get input from external agencies.

'We thought we should rethink the approach for engaging and receiving responses from our suppliers, because the standard Request For Proposal process seemed so 1980s,' recalls Bianco. 'So instead, we invited six suppliers of the Bank to participate in a three-day Hothouse event.'

The event was kicked off by the Bank's Chief Information Officer painting the vision of the employee of the future. Employees were then on hand to speak to each supplier, where each participant had a chance to understand employees' current pain points and future needs. The three-day event culminated in several fully functioning prototypes being presented to four executive judges, with each prototype having been tested by employees as the development progressed.

'Not only was the process a great way for suppliers to showcase their skills and ideas,' says Bianco, 'But it also provided the bank with high quality deliverables, exceptional thinking due to the competitiveness of the environment, and a much quicker process. And on top of all that, we were able to receive prototypes that we could touch and feel rather than a response in a word document.'

★★★

Encouraging participation in company innovation award programs is another way to demonstrate to everyone that their opinion matters. At Pfizer, Wendy Mayer, vice president of worldwide innovation, says they learned this the hard way with their Dare to Try program awards, which are given out quarterly at a corporate level. 'It used to just be my small innovation team that judged the entries', recalls Mayer. 'We would divvy up the nominations and we would say, "Okay. What do we think are the five most innovative things happening across Pfizer?" It was really challenging because we clearly were not experts in a lot of these areas. It was challenging to try to really understand what these teams were doing and we always questioned whether we were really speaking for the broader organisation. Were we identifying things that people in other parts of the organisation would say, "Yes! I'm proud that that's one of the five most innovative things this quarter that's happening at Pfizer"'.

As a result of these concerns, Mayer and her team decided to crowdsource the process. The way this works is that every nominated innovation is listed and described on an organisation-wide technology platform. Everyone is encouraged to go in and have a look. Individuals can look at one project or a hundred projects—whatever they feel like. There are different dimensions that each innovation is evaluated against and an average score is calculated.

Moving to the crowdsource model was a huge win for the awards program in terms of engaging the wider organisation in the process. 'In the first week, we had over five thousand colleagues evaluate projects, which is tremendous', explains Mayer.

Through the crowdsourced decision-making process, the top 25 ideas are identified. Following this, Mayer's team of champions identify which five out of those 25 should get the award. 'It enables us to get broader organisational input', says Mayer. 'We've also heard feedback from across the organisation that the people evaluating these projects are so impressed with the work that's happening across the company. It's a way to inspire people and give them broader exposure.'

## KEY POINTS

- Inviting everyone in an organisation to contribute to innovation is important in building a strong innovation culture.

- Having a best-practice innovation process that is clearly communicated to the rest of the organisation will help people understand how they can easily contribute to innovation.

- Democratising innovation at the front end (especially around identifying customer frustrations and generating ideas to solve those frustrations) has been found to be the most effective way to approach innovation.

- When you get to the back end of innovation — prototyping and implementing solutions — the best approach is to compartmentalise to ensure that action actually happens.

- Using an innovation rewards program and inviting people to vote on their favourite ideas is another way of driving participation in innovation across an entire company.

# CHAPTER 14
# PHYSICAL ENVIRONMENT

Turning up the background noise, and other strategies for enhancing innovation

Not many companies agonise over their physical environment the way Circus Oz does. The design of its new office and rehearsal space in the edgy Melbourne suburb of Collingwood was a ten-year process. And when you walk in, you get the sense that it was all worth it.

Many of the decisions in creating the new space were based on how the company could increase collaboration. Circus Oz's previous home was an old heritage-listed post office and an old heritage-listed Navy drill hall that happened to be adjoining. The buildings were connected by a little corridor and tiny courtyard where the bins were kept. The performers kept to the rehearsal space in the Navy drill hall and the office staff stayed in the post office. Rather than encourage collaboration and innovation, the space inhibited it.

In direct contrast, the new space is built around a huge central rehearsal space that breeds collaboration. Every workstation is no more than 4 metres from a window that looks onto the main rehearsal space.'It means that everyone from finance and marketing, through to the receptionist, can stand up from their desk and just take two or three steps and look through a glass window and go, "Oh, right. That's what they're working on today"', explains Mike Finch, artistic director and joint CEO. 'And we deliberately didn't completely soundproof the rehearsal space, because we wanted people to be able to hear what's going on in the background — so when the band is playing in the building you can hear it as a really dull thudding.'

The kitchen overlooks a three-storey atrium that runs down the spine of the building. When the performers go up to the kitchen to take their lunch break, the office staff take theirs too, so they all sit and eat together. Finch describes the conversations that now happen because of interaction that the new design encourages. An admin person will say to a performer, "I saw you doing that thing down there. It was really interesting. Can I come and take some photos of that for the latest Twitter post?" Marketing starts to talk to acrobatics and then ideas come up organically. They go, "Oh, that reminded me of this YouTube clip that I just saw last night", and they tell the acrobat about it and the acrobat goes out and tries it that afternoon and then a new idea appears.'

Circus Oz's office has become an unofficial hub for the contemporary circus community. 'When someone comes to Melbourne from a travelling show', says Finch, 'they will drop in at Circus Oz. You get a sort of cross-pollination and a disruptive effect from outsiders who have been working in a different context. They might have been in a dance acrobatics show in Europe for the last two years, but they've dropped in to see the work that's going on in the rehearsal space. People then fire off some brand new idea that wouldn't have occurred to anyone working in isolation.'

★★★

While a ten-year design process for an office is at the extreme end of things, most offices unfortunately receive little to no thought about how the design will affect people's innovativeness, productivity and wellbeing. Nine out of ten offices I visit through my work at Inventium are grey, dull and illuminated by horribly artificial fluorescent lighting. Meeting rooms are often characterised by windowless white or pale grey walls, sparse 'decorations' and beige furniture. Not the kind of environment that inspires creativity.

And interestingly, in many of the major meta-analyses that have been conducted into what drives a culture of innovation, one variable has been noticeably absent: the physical environment. Yet there is a significant body of research that clearly demonstrates the impact that our physical working environment has on our work experience and on our ability to think and perform in certain ways. As such, this final chapter focuses on how you can begin to manipulate and change your physical working environment so that it becomes one that fosters, rather than hinders, innovation.

★★★

Of all the ways to change your physical environment for the better, those involving nature have received the most attention. In one such study, Marlon Nieuwenhuis, from Cardiff University, and her colleagues were keen to investigate the impact of greenery on people's happiness and productivity at work. In an initial study, they decked out half an office in greenery and left the other half bland. Three weeks later, employees in the green half said they had felt more focused and productive as a result of the plants.

In a follow-up study, the researchers installed plants in a call centre, so that every single employee had a view of at least one large plant. Three months later employees reported feeling significantly happier and more engaged at work, compared with their counterparts on a different floor who had not received any greenery.

In a final experiment, the researchers invited 33 people to complete a task in either a green or non-green office environment.

Those in the green office completed the task significantly faster and without any additional errors. Nieuwenhuis and her colleagues found that overall, productivity could be increased by up to 15 per cent simply by bringing in a few plants—a finding that is extraordinarily easy for offices to implement.

Research shows that exposure to nature also has a beneficial effect on creativity. Ruth Atchley, from the University of Kansas, and her colleagues studied a group of people who were going on a four-day hike without any access to technology. Half of the hikers were asked to complete a creative problem-solving task prior to their hike, and the other half were asked to complete it on day four of the hike. People who had experienced four days' immersion in nature, without any technological distractions, performed 50 per cent better in the creative problem-solving task. This study emphasises the important role that nature can play in creativity. Taking breaks from technology can also be beneficial.

The beneficial role that exposure to nature can play in lowering stress levels which, in turn increases creativity, has also been well documented by researchers. Stress levels can also be lowered by physical elements such as lighting and views of the outside world. Julian Thayer, from Ohio State University, and several of his colleagues investigated the impact that the office environment has on stress levels. Thayer recruited 60 people who worked in either a traditional office with poor views and lighting, or in a more modern building that had better views and natural light. The researchers found that employees working in the office space with poor views and dimmer lighting experienced higher levels of cortisol, a hormone that is released in response to stress.

★★★

Ravi Mehta, from the University of British Columbia, and his colleagues were interested in the impact of noise on creativity. Sixty-five students were brought into the lab to complete a creative problem-solving test. The students were split into four groups: high noise, medium noise, low noise and no noise. Prior to the experiment, the researchers had created an ambient sound mix from a combination of real noise from cafés and the street. Mehta and his colleagues found that those in the medium noise group (70 decibels) performed significantly better than those in the low, high or no noise groups. Interestingly, after the study, participants' moods (for example, whether they were happy or sad) were measured to rule out their effect on the results. The researchers found that background noise had an effect regardless of participants' moods.

In a series of follow-up experiments involving tasks such as generating new ideas for a mattress manufacturer, it was found that the medium noise-level group outperformed all other noise-level groups, with their ideas being judged as significantly more creative. In addition, the researchers measured participants' processing disfluency (which is essentially a person's level of distraction), as this had been shown in research to lead to abstract processing and thus greater creativity. Immediately after the task, people were asked how distracted they had felt during the activity. As suspected, those in the medium noise group had experienced a greater amount of distraction than those in lower noise groups.

In one final experiment, Mehta explored whether a moderate level of ambient noise also affect people's likelihood of adopting innovations. To explore this, 68 students were brought into a cubicle located in the student lounge area on campus and were presented with various choices of traditional versus innovative products. Noise level was also monitored, given that it was a real-life environment (as opposed to a lab). As hypothesised, it was found that when exposed to a moderate level of background noise, people were significantly more likely to adopt more innovative products than more traditional ones.

... when exposed to a moderate level of background noise, people were significantly more likely to adopt more innovative products than more traditional ones.

When thinking about your office, consider zoning off areas with different sound levels. While silence is needed for certain types of work (such as highly focused work, or teleconferences), consider having some parts of the office where there is a moderate level of noise for those involved in work requiring innovation. Mehta's research suggests that 70 decibels is a moderate sound level—it's similar to the level of sound you would hear when walking down a typical city street.

★★★

The past few years have produced some conflicting research into the effects of colour. Janet McCoy, from Arizona State University, set out to investigate the type of environment people seek out when they have creative work. Amongst other things, McCoy found that participants were likely to avoid cooler colours and be more attracted to warmer colours for creative spaces. In a second study, McCoy found that people produced significantly more original and interesting collages when working an environment that had different shades of colour than they did when working in a monochromatic environment.

In more recent years researchers have found that blue and green also have a positive impact on innovation due to their association with nature—when people are exposed to either of those colours, they report feeling more relaxed. For example, several researchers from the University of Munich brought a group of 65 people into the lab to complete a creative problem-solving task. However, before engaging in the task, some people were shown a green login screen while others were shown a white screen. The researchers found that those seeing a green screen performed about 20 per cent better on the creative thinking task.

In further studies, green was pitted against red, blue and grey and emerged every time as the winner. The researchers suggested that the colour green was so impactful in enhancing creativity because it reminded people of nature—and, as discussed earlier in this chapter, the benefits of nature to innovation (not to mention productivity) has been consistently shown.

While studies into colour are somewhat contradictory, what we can be sure of is that some colour is better than no colour.

So rather than settle for a drab, grey office, throw in some colour wherever you can.

★★★

There is a lot of research into the impact of exposing ourselves to diverse and unexpected stimuli. Maria Clapham from Drake University found that people who were exposed to a list of 60 unrelated sentences performed significantly better on an idea-generation task than those who had not seen the diverse stimuli. These findings suggest that exposure to lots of unrelated information gets the creative juices flowing. Indeed, the more thoughts and experiences you have floating around in your brain, the greater your chance of having creative and lateral thoughts.

After educating many of our clients about the types of physical environments that foster innovation, Inventium moved office at the beginning of 2015. We set about the exciting task of practising what we have been preaching for so many years.

Finding the right space proved to be the first challenge. We knew we wanted a place oozing with natural light, which is surprisingly challenging to find in Melbourne's CBD. We wanted a place with personality, as opposed to one of the generic offices that line most cities. And high ceilings were on our wish list too. I inspected over 40 office sites before finding our new home. And when I found it, I knew it was for us.

When we signed the lease on our new home it was a rectangular shell, but a shell that had oodles of natural light, beautiful four-metre-high ceilings, and was in a quirky old building. As an added bonus, it happened to be above one of Melbourne's most delicious restaurants, Chin Chin.

*(continued)*

We worked with a designer to bring the shell to life. We brought in a street artist named Tunni to write random 'did you know' facts all over our walls (we spent days finding the most unusual and reaction-provoking facts). We sourced over 50 different plants (mostly real, although some fake) to scatter throughout the office, including a few that hang from our ceiling. We all work on two big communal tables, which keeps background noise to a moderate level and makes for easy collaboration. And we created several casual meeting areas for when people needed to break away from the crowd. I know that I speak on behalf of my team when I say it's the best and most energising office any of us has ever worked in.

★★★

While you have hopefully found the suggestions made in this chapter so far very practical, I am aware that some readers might also be feeling a bit helpless if you have no authority to make major changes to your office building. If that is the case, then this final piece of research should be useful. Researchers from the University of Exeter in the UK examined whether giving people control over how they decorate their workspace increased their productivity and satisfaction at work. They found that those who did have control over furnishings and decor were 32 per cent more productive than their non-empowered colleagues.

Unfortunately, some organisations are unmoved by this kind of research. In 2012, when several thousand BHP Billiton staff came to work at the company's West Australian headquarters, an 11-page document gave very clear instructions on how the office and desk space were to be used. Under the company's 'clear desk' policy, the only items that were allowed to remain on employees' desks at the end of each day were their computer monitor, a keyboard, a mouse and mouse pad, a telephone handset and headset, one A5 photo frame and ergonomic equipment. And in case that wasn't clear enough, the document included a photo to show what a clear desk looks like. Staff were forbidden from bringing in their own pot plant or even personalising their screensaver.

In direct contrast, Christine Gilroy, group general manager of innovation at construction company Mirvac, ensured that employees at Mirvac had full control over several spaces that were designated for innovation. After learning about some of the core principles that lead to creative workspaces, Gilroy realised that their offices were almost in opposition to these principles. In response to this, Gilroy set the challenge of transforming the rooms into amazing creative spaces.

A call was sent out for volunteers who were keen to transform the spaces. They were given four weeks and $15000 to make the transformation happen. 'It was like *The Block* but for corporates', explains Gilroy. 'We got a really diverse team of people who had never worked together before. Each brought different strengths to the project. While we did have some volunteers from construction and design, we also had lots of accountants and personal assistants and all sorts of different people.'

Gilroy had no idea what was going to happen, and prepared herself for a disaster after one of the team's construction works accidentally triggered a call to the fire brigade. But the end result was some amazing creative spaces that are now almost fully booked for various innovation projects and workshops. 'There were so many benefits from the project. Not only did we get these great spaces but it showed what happens when you empower a team of people. It was an opportunity for them to showcase all the other talents that they had outside of work.'

In a similar vein to Mirvac, the Australian arm of global pharmaceutical company AbbVie made the conscious decision to take a collaborative approach to an office move and redesign for their 300-odd staff. Managing Director Kirsten O'Doherty invited people to form teams to work on different elements of the office move—from the physical environment, to culture change, through to going paperless.

'We had about 60 people across the business involved in one of the teams', recalls O'Doherty. 'They actually did all the work. The teams made all the changes for going paperless, they designed and picked a lot of the arrangements for furniture, and had input into the entire office layout.'

One of the distinctive features of the new offices is its zoning. While the entire office consists of hot-desks, part of the office is a 'quiet' area for those who need to get away from the noise to focus. Other parts of the office are designed for talk and collaboration. And the kitchen was centrally located—it's a place where everyone comes together for meals and various events.

'We wanted to create an environment where you have people bumping into each other all the time. We have definitely seen a really major change in that someone could be sitting next to a person in pharmacovigilance one day, someone from finance the next day, and someone from medical the day after. Everybody moves around all the time and people have made very genuine comments about how much more connected they feel. How much more they feel they know about the business. How many more conversations they're having. And fewer emails.

'To encourage the collaboration and 'bumping into' effect, we have a barista who works in the kitchen. It's now the first place most people go to in the morning and if you were to visit the office at 8.30 or 9 am, you would see everyone's in there, chatting, catching up with each other and getting a coffee.'

# KEY POINTS

- Bringing nature, which can include anything from a view of nature to a pot plant on your desk, into your workspace not only has a positive impact on innovation, but also on productivity and general wellbeing.

- A moderate level of noise has been found to enhance innovation, as it acts as a mild distraction, which fosters creativity.

- Both warm and cold colours (and green specifically) have been shown to have a positive impact on creating a culture of innovation.

- Being exposed to diverse stimuli enhances creativity, so think about how you can bring new and unexpected stimuli into the work environment.

- Views and natural lighting are both important aspects to enhancing the physical environment.

- Create central points of collaboration to increase the chances of people 'bumping into' each other.

# WHAT NOW?

This book examined the 14 biggest drivers of an innovation culture. Focusing on 14 different elements all at once can seem like a mammoth task! So rather than trying to do it all straight away, I recommend that you revisit your results from the Innovation Culture Audit that you completed at the start of the book. Identify your three lowest-scoring areas as the starting point. Focusing on three of the 14 areas is a manageable amount of work to start with, and you can easily get to the other variables later on.

Once you have your three priority areas, it's worth going back over some of the real-life examples of how other organisations are bringing those variables to life. At Inventium we have a motto about good ideas. We say 'steal with respect'. By this, we don't mean shoplift or steal someone's IP without formally acknowledging them. What we do mean is that if another company has come up with a great way of encouraging risk-taking, for example, then feel free to adapt what they have done to your own context rather than feeling like you have to reinvent the wheel.

For example, if risk-taking is an area in which your organisation scores low, as we find many do, you might want to adopt the Tata Group's idea and have your own Dare to Try awards to recognise innovations that didn't quite hit the mark commercially but did contain some great learnings for your company (see chapter 11).

If resourcing is an issue for your organisation, why not take Adobe's Kickbox idea and use it, just like Nestlé did (see chapter 9).

Try not to feel discouraged if you are not the CEO or director of innovation and perhaps have no decision-making authority. You don't need to start big to make an impact. There are plenty of opportunities and ideas in the book that you can easily implement at an individual or team level. For example, the simple act of putting a pot plant on your desk will enhance innovation—both for you, and for anyone else who happens to have a view of your desk.

Changing a culture won't happen overnight, but rather than purchasing a foosball table and some beanbags and hoping for the best, you are now at least armed with the precise science of how to actually create a culture where innovation will thrive.

# REFERENCES

## Introduction

Hunter, ST, Bedell, KE & Mumford, MD 2007. 'Climate for creativity: A quantitative review', *Creativity Research Journal*, 19(1), 69–90.

## Part I

### Chapter 1: Challenge

Amabile, TM & Gryszkiewicz, SS 1987. 'Creativity in the R&D laboratory', Center for Creative Leadership, USA.

Amabile, TM, Conti, R, Coon, H, Lazenby, J et al. 1996. 'Assessing the work environment for creativity', *Academy of Management Journal*, 39(5), 1154–1184.

Bartlett, CA, Hall, BJ & Bennett, NS 2008. 'GE's imagination breakthroughs: The Evo project', *Harvard Business Review*, 30 June.

Csikszentmihalyi, M 2008. *Flow: The psychology of optimal experience*, Harper Perennial Modern Classics, USA.

Csikszentmihalyi, M & LeFevre, J 1989. 'Optimal experience in work and leisure', *Journal of Personality and Social Psychology*, 56, 815–822.

Donner, J & Csikszentmihalyi, M 1992. 'Transforming stress into flow', *Executive Excellence*, 9, 16–17.

Hatcher, L, Ross, TL & Collins, D 1989. 'Prosocial behavior, job complexity, and suggestion contribution under gainsharing plans', *Journal of Applied Behavioral Science* (3), 231.

Hunter, ST, Bedell, KE & Mumford, MD 2007. 'Climate for creativity: A quantitative review', *Creativity Research Journal*, 19(1), 69–90.

Lafley, AG & Charan, R 2008. *The game-changer: How you can drive revenue and profit growth with innovation*, Crown Business, USA.

Oldham, GR & Cummings, A 1996. 'Employee creativity: Personal and contextual factors at work', *Academy of Management Journal*, 39(3), 607–634.

Yerkes, RM & Dodson, JD 1908. 'The relation of strength of stimulus to rapidity of habit-formation', *Journal of Comparative Neurology and Psychology*, 18, 459–482.

## Further reading

Constantine, A & Andy, L 2000. 'Enhancing organisational creativity: The process of perpetual challenging', *Management Decision*, 38(10), 734–742.

Cummings, A & Oldham, GR 1997. 'Enhancing creativity: Managing work contexts for the high potential employee', *California Management Review*, 40(1), 22–38.

Ekvall, G 1983. 'Climate, structure and innovativeness of organizations (Report 1)', FArådet, the Swedish Council for Management and Organizational Behaviour.

Hackman, JR, Oldham, G, Janson, R & Purdy, K 1975. 'A new strategy for job enrichment', *California Management Review*, 17(4), 57–71.

Ohly, S & Fritz, C 2010. 'Work characteristics, challenge appraisal, creativity, and proactive behavior: A multi-level study', *Journal of Organizational Behavior*, 31(4), 543–565.

Oldham, GR & Cummings, A 1996. 'Employee creativity: Personal and contextual factors at work', *Academy of Management Journal*, 39(3), 607–634.

Parameter, SM & Garber, JD 1971. 'Creative scientists rate creativity factors', *Research Management*, 14(1), 65–70.

Pelz, DC & Andrews, FM 1978. *Scientists in organizations: Productive climates for research and development*, University of Michigan, USA.

Robinson, AG & Stern, S 1997. *Corporate creativity: How innovation and improvement actually happen*, Berrett-Koehler Publishers, USA.

Tierney, P & Farmer, SM 2002. 'Creative self-efficacy: Its potential antecedents and relationship to creative performance', *Academy of Management Journal*, 45(6), 1137–1148.

## Chapter 2: Autonomy

Amabile, TM 1998. 'How to kill creativity'. Retrieved from http://www.achieveglobal.ro/wp-content/uploads/2012/11/How-to-kill-creativity.pdf.

Amabile, TM & Gitomer, J 1984. 'Children's artistic creativity effects of choice in task materials', *Personality and Social Psychology Bulletin*, 10(2), 209–215.

Amabile, TM, Conti, R, Coon, H, Lazenby, J et al. 1996. 'Assessing the work environment for creativity', *Academy of Management Journal*, 39(5), 1154–1184.

Axtell, CM, Holman, DJ, Unsworth, KL, Wall, TD et al. 2000. 'Shopfloor innovation: Facilitating the suggestion and implementation of ideas', *Journal of Occupational and Organizational Psychology*, 73(3), 265–285.

Bock, L 2015. *Work Rules! Insights from inside Google that will transform how you live and lead*, Hodder and Stoughton, UK.

Chang, JW, Huang, DW & Choi, JN 2012. 'Is task autonomy beneficial for creativity? Prior task experience and self-control as boundary conditions', *Social Behavior and Personality: An International Journal*, 40(5), 705–724.

da Costa, S, Páez, D, Sánchez, F, Gondim, S et al. 2014. 'Factors favoring innovation in organizations: An integration of meta-analyses', *Revista de Psicología del Trabajo y de las Organizaciones*, 30(2), 67–74.

Greenberg, E 1992. 'Creativity, autonomy, and evaluation of creative work: Artistic workers in organizations', *Journal of Creative Behavior*, 26(2), 75–80.

Hastings, R 2009. 'Netflix culture: freedom & responsibility', slide presentation, 1 August. Retrieved from http://www.slideshare.net/reed2001/culture-1798664.

Krause, DE 2004. 'Influence-based leadership as a determinant of the inclination to innovate and of innovation-related behaviors: An empirical investigation', *Leadership Quarterly*, 15(1), 79–102.

Levesque, C & Pelletier, LG 2003. 'On the investigation of primed and chronic autonomous and heteronomous motivational orientations', *Personality and Social Psychology Bulletin*, 29(12), 1570–1584.

Locke, R, Kochan, T, Romis, M & Qin, F 2007. 'Beyond corporate codes of conduct: Work organization and labour standards at Nike's suppliers', *International Labour Review*, 146(1–2), 21–40.

'The world's most innovative companies: #27 — Netflix', *Forbes*, 2015. Retrieved from http://www.forbes.com/companies/netflix/.

## Further reading

Binnewies, C & Gromer, M 2012. 'Creativity and innovation at work: The role of work characteristics and personal initiative', *Psicothema*, 24(1), 100–105.

Joo, BK, Yang, B & McLean, GN 2014. 'Employee creativity: The effects of perceived learning culture, leader–member exchange quality, job autonomy, and proactivity', *Human Resource Development International*, 17(3), 297–317.

## Chapter 3: Recognition

Amabile, TM, Schatzel, EA, Moneta, GB & Kramer, SJ 2004. 'Leader behaviors and the work environment for creativity: Perceived leader support', *The Leadership Quarterly*, 15(1), 5–32.

Atkinson, JW 1964. *An introduction to motivation*, Van Nostrand, USA.

Baer, M, Oldham, GR & Cummings, A 2003. 'Rewarding creativity: When does it really matter?', *Leadership Quarterly*, 14(4), 569–586.

Blackwell, L, Trzesniewski, K & Dweck, CS 2007. 'Implicit theories of intelligence predict achievement across an adolescent transition: A longitudinal study and an intervention', *Child Development*, 78, 246–263.

Deci, EL & Ryan, RM 2000. 'The "what" and the "why" of goal pursuits: Human needs and the self-determination of behavior', *Psychological Inquiry*, 11, 227–268.

Deci, EL, Koestner, R & Ryan, RM 1999. 'A meta-analytic review of experiments examining the effects of extrinsic rewards on intrinsic motivation', *Psychological Bulletin*, 125, 627–668.

Hewett, R & Conway, N 2015. 'The undermining effect revisited: The salience of everyday verbal rewards and self-determined motivation', *Journal of Organizational Behavior*. Available from: http://onlinelibrary.wiley.com/doi/10.1002/job.2051/abstract

Intuit, 2012. 'Say thank you. Repeat eight million times'. Retrieved from http://www.intuitatwork2012.com/thanking.html.

Mueller, CM & Dweck, CS 1998. 'Praise for intelligence can undermine children's motivation and performance', *Journal of Personality and Social Psychology*, 75(1), 33–52.

Shepherd, DA & DeTienne, DR 2005. 'Prior knowledge, potential financial reward, and opportunity identification', *Entrepreneurship Theory and Practice*, 29(1), 91–112.

Zhou, Y, Zhang, Y & Montoro-Sánchez, Á 2011. 'Utilitarianism or romanticism: The effect of rewards on employees' innovative behaviour', *International Journal of Manpower*, 32(1), 81–98.

# Further reading

Hoarty, N, Gopal, G & Elwood, LP 2013. 'Using reward systems to motivate employees for innovation', *Global Education Journal*, 2013(3).

Malaviya, P & Wadhwa, S 2005. 'Innovation management in organizational context: An empirical study', *Global Journal of Flexible Systems Management*, 6(2), 1–14.

Martins, EC & Terblanche, F 2003. 'Building organisational culture that stimulates creativity and innovation', *European Journal of Innovation Management*, 6(1), 64–74.

Sousa, C & Luís, C 2013. 'Innovation, creativity and reward practices in academic spin-offs: The case of the IST spin-off community', *Portuguese Journal of Social Science*, 12(3), 263–286.

Volmer, J, Spurk, D & Niessen, C 2012. 'Leader–member exchange (LMX), job autonomy, and creative work involvement', *Leadership Quarterly*, 23(3), 456–465.

# Part II

Hülsheger, UR, Anderson, N & Salgado, JF 2009. 'Team level predictors of innovation at work: A comprehensive meta-analysis spanning three decades of research', *Journal of Applied Psychology*, 94(5), 1128–1145.

## Chapter 4: Debate

Bock, L 2015. *Work Rules! Insights from inside Google that will transform how you live and lead*, Hodder and Stoughton, UK.

Clapham, MM 2001. 'The effects of affect manipulation and information exposure on divergent thinking', *Creativity Research Journal*, 13, 335–350.

Hülsheger, UR, Anderson, N & Salgado, JF 2009. 'Team level predictors of innovation at work: A comprehensive meta-analysis spanning three decades of research', *Journal of Applied Psychology*, 94(5), 1128–1145.

Hunsberger, B 2009. 'Nike, Wieden+Kennedy haul in ad of the decade awards', *The Oregonian*, 17 December. Retrieved from http://www.oregonlive.com/business/index.ssf/2009/12/nike_wiedenkennedy_haul_in_ad.html.

Kwoh, L 2011.'Reverse mentoring cracks workplace', *The Wall Street Journal*, 28 November. Retrieved from http://www.wsj.com/articles/SB10001424052970203764804577060051461094004.

Rivera, LA 2012. 'Hiring as cultural matching: The case of elite professional service firms', *American Sociological Review*, 77(6), 999–1022.

Stackpole, B 2014. 'IT puts millennials to work, as mentors', *Computerworld*, 19 August. Retrieved from http://www.computerworld.com/article/2491199/it-management-it-puts-millennials-to-work-as-mentors.html.

## Chapter 5: Team supportiveness

Ainsworth, M 1967. *Infancy in Uganda: Infant care and the growth of love*, John Hopkins Press, UK.

Ainsworth, M 1963. 'The development of infant-mother interaction among the Ganda', in BM Foss (ed.), *Determinants of infant behavior*, Wiley, USA.

Amabile, TM & Gryszkiewicz SS 1987. 'Creativity in the R&D laboratory', Center for Creative Leadership, USA.

Bowlby, J 1969. *Attachment and Loss*, Basic Books, USA.

Bretherton, I 1992.'The origins of attachment theory: John Bowlby and Mary Ainsworth', *Developmental Psychology*, 28(5), 759–775.

Hoegl, M & Gemuenden, HG 2001. 'Teamwork quality and the success of innovative projects: A theoretical concept and empirical evidence', *Organization Science*, 12(4), 435–449.

Hülsheger, UR, Anderson, N & Salgado, JF 2009. 'Team level predictors of innovation at work: A comprehensive meta-analysis spanning three decades of research', *Journal of Applied Psychology*, 94(5), 1128–1145.

Klein, M 1932. *The psycho-analysis of children*, Hogarth Press, UK.

West, MA & Wallace, M 1991. 'Innovation in health care teams', *European Journal of Social Psychology*, 21, 303–315.

## Chapter 6: Collaboration

Bernstein, ES, Gino, F & Staats, BR 2014. 'Opening the Valve: From software to hardware', *Harvard Business Review*, 25 August. Retrieved from https://hbr.org/product/opening-the-valve-from-software-to-hardware-a/415015-PDF-ENG.

Briody, EK & Erickson, KC 2014. 'Success despite the silos: System-wide innovation and collaboration', *Business Anthropology*, 30, 30–54.

Conditt, J 2014. 'Steam has 75 million active users, Valve announces at Dev Days', Engadget, 15 January. Retrieved from http://www.engadget.com/2014/01/15/steam-has-75-million-active-users-valve-announces-at-dev-days/.

Ewalt, DM 2012. 'Valve's Gabe Newell is the newest video game billionaire', *Forbes*, 7 March. Retrieved from http://www.forbes.com/sites/davidewalt/2012/03/07/valve-gabe-newell-billionaire/.

Hirst, G, Van Knippenberg, D, Zhou, J, Quintane, E et al. 2015. 'Heard it through the grapevine: Indirect networks and employee creativity', *Journal of Applied Psychology*, 100(2), 567.

Hunter, ST, Bedell, KE & Mumford, MD 2007. 'Climate for creativity: A quantitative review', *Creativity Research Journal*, 19(1), 69–90.

Lapierre, J & Giroux, VP 2003. 'Creativity and work environment in a high-tech context', *Creativity & Innovation Management*, 12(1), 11–23.

Mueller, V, Rosenbusch, N & Bausch, A 2013. 'Success patterns of exploratory and exploitative innovation: A meta–analysis of the influence of institutional factors', *Journal of Management*, 39(6), 1606–1636.

Ross, C 2014. 'New York ad agency Anomaly departs from the norm to bring success to clients', Mediajobs.com, 4 March. Retrieved from http://mediajobs.com/new-york-ad-agency-anomaly-departs-norm-bring-success-clients/4150/.

Valve 2008. 'Half-life is 10 today', media release, 19 November. Retrieved from http://store.steampowered.com/news/2039/.

Valve 2012. *Valve Handbook for New Employees*. Retrieved from http://www.valvesoftware.com/company/Valve_Handbook_LowRes.pdf.

## Further reading

Amabile, TM & Gryszkiewicz, SS 1987. 'Creativity in the R&D Laboratory', Center for Creative Leadership, USA.

Briody, EK, Trotter II, RT & Meerwarth II, TL 2010. *Transforming culture: Creating and sustaining a better manufacturing organization*, Palgrave Macmillan, USA.

Burke, WW 1989. 'Culture Instrument', working paper. Columbia University, USA.

Hoegl, M & Gemuenden, HG 2001. 'Teamwork. quality and the success of innovative projects: A theoretical concept and empirical evidence', *Organization science*, 12(4), 435–449.

Hurley, RF & Hult, GTM 1998. 'Innovation, market orientation, and organizational learning: An integration and empirical examination', *Journal of Marketing*, 62(3), 42–54.

Michael, A 1991. 'Innovation in health care teams', *European Journal of Social Psychology*, 21, 303–315.

Paulus, PB & Nijstad, BA 2003. *Group creativity: Innovation through collaboration*, Oxford University Press, UK.

Pierce, JL & Delbecq, AL 1977. 'Organization structure, individual attitudes and innovation', *Academy of Management Review*, 2(1), 27–37.

# Part III

## Chapter 7: Supervisor support

Amabile, TM & Conti, R 1999. 'Changes in the work environment for creativity during downsizing', *Academy of Management Journal*, 42, 630–640.

Amabile, TM, Schatzel, EA, Moneta, GB & Kramer, SJ 2004. 'Leader behaviors and the work environment for creativity: Perceived leader support', *Leadership Quarterly*, 15(1), 5–32.

Jaussi, KS, Randel, AE & Dionne, SD 2007. 'I am, I think I can, and I do: The role of personal identity, self-efficacy, and cross-application of experiences in creativity at work', *Creativity Research Journal*, 19, 247–258.

Oldham, GR & Cummings, A 1996. 'Employee creativity: Personal and contextual factors at work', *Academy of Management Journal*, 39(3), 607–634.

Ramus, CA & Steger, U 2000. 'The roles of supervisory support behaviours and environmental policy in employee 'ecoinitiatives' at leading-edge European companies', *Academy of Management Journal*, 43(4), 605–626.

Redmond, MR, Mumford, MD & Teach, R 1993. 'Putting creativity to work: Effects of leader behavior on subordinate creativity', *Organizational Behavior & Human Decision Processes*, 55(1), 120–151.

Tierney, P, Farmer, SM & Graen, GB 1999. 'An examination of leadership and employee creativity: The relevance of traits and relationships,' *Personnel Psychology*, 52, 591–620.

## Further reading

Amabile, TM, Conti, R, Coon, H, Lazenby, J et al. 1996. 'Assessing the work environment for creativity', *Academy of Management Journal*, 39(5), 1154–1184.

Andrews, FM & Farris, GF 1967. 'Supervisory practices and innovation in scientific teams', *Personnel Psychology*, 20(4), 497–515.

Scott, SG & Bruce, RA 1994. 'Determinants of innovative behaviour: A path model of individual innovation in the workplace', *Academy of Management Journal*, 37(3), 580–607.

Stahl, MJ & Koser, MC 1978. 'Weighted productivity in R & D: Some associated individual and organizational variables', *Engineering Management, IEEE Transactions on*, 25(1), 20, 24.

### Chapter 8: Senior leader support

Dyer, J, Gregersen, H & Christensen, C 2013. *The innovator's DNA: Mastering the five skills of disruptive innovators*, Harvard Business Press, USA.

Hunter, ST, Bedell, KE & Mumford, MD 2007. 'Climate for creativity: A quantitative review', *Creativity Research Journal*, 19(1), 69–90.

Mueller, V, Rosenbusch, N & Bausch, A 2013. 'Success patterns of exploratory and exploitative innovation: A meta-analysis of the influence of institutional factors', *Journal of Management*, 39(6), 1606–1636.

## Further reading

Amabile, TM, Conti, R, Coon, H, Lazenby, J et al. 1996. 'Assessing the work environment for creativity', *Academy of Management Journal*, 39(5), 1154–1184.

Amabile, TM, Schatzel, EA, Moneta, GB & Kramer, SJ 2004. 'Leader behaviors and the work environment for creativity: Perceived leader support', *Leadership Quarterly*, 15(1), 5–32.

Oldham, GR & Cummings, A 1996. 'Employee creativity: Personal and contextual factors at work', *Academy of Management Journal*, 39(3), 607–634.

References

Redmond, MR, Mumford, MD & Teach, R 1993. 'Putting creativity to work: Effects of leader behavior on subordinate creativity', *Organizational Behavior & Human Decision Processes*, 55(1), 120–151.

### Chapter 9: Resourcing

Burkus, D 2015. 'Inside Adobe's innovation kit', *Harvard Business Review*, February 23. Retrieved from https://hbr.org/2015/02/inside-adobes-innovation-kit.

Carr, A 2012. 'Paul Graham: Why Y Combinator replaces the traditional corporation', *Fast Company*, 22 February. Retrieved from http://www.fastcompany.com/1818523/paul-graham-why-y-combinator-replaces-traditional-corporation.

Graham, P 2012. 'How Y Combinator started', blog entry, March 15. Retrieved from http://old.ycombinator.com/start.html.

Katila, R & Shane, S 2005. 'When does lack of resources make new firms innovative?', *Academy of Management Journal*, 48(5), 814–829.

Martín, P, Salanova, M & Peiró, JM 2007. 'Job demands, job resources and individual innovation at work: Going beyond Karasek's model?', *Psicothema*, 19(4), 621–626.

Scott, K 2012. 'The LinkedIn incubator', blog entry, December 7. Retrieved from http://blog.linkedin.com/2012/12/07/linkedin-incubator/.

Tate, R 2012. 'LinkedIn gone wild: "20 percent time" to tinker spreads beyond Google', *Wired*, 6 December. Retrieved from http://www.wired.com/2012/12/llinkedin-20-percent-time/.

## Further reading

Castiaux, A & Paque, S 2009. 'Participative innovation: When innovation becomes everyone's business', *International Journal of Entrepreneurship and Innovation Management*, 10(2), 111-121.

Hewitt-Dundas, N 2006. 'Resource and capability constraints to innovation in small and large plants', *Small Business Economics*, 26(3), 257–277.

Kristensson, P, Magnusson, PR & Matthing, J 2002. 'Users as a hidden resource for creativity: Findings from an experimental study on user involvement', *Creativity and Innovation Management*, 11(1), 55–61.

### Chapter 10: Goal clarity

Amabile, T & Kramer, S 2011. *The progress principle: Using small wins to ignite joy, engagement, and creativity at work*, Harvard Business Press, USA.

da Costa, S, Páez, D, Sánchez, F, Gondim, S et al. 2014. 'Factors favoring innovation in organizations: An integration of meta-analyses', *Revista de Psicología del Trabajo y de las Organizaciones*, 30(2), 67–74.

Hoegl, M & Parboteeah, KP 2003. 'Goal setting and team performance in innovative projects: On the moderating role of teamwork quality', *Small Group Research*, 34(1), 3–19.

## Further reading

Carson, PP & Carson, KD 1993. 'Managing creativity enhancement through goal-setting and feedback', *Journal of Creative Behavior*, 27(1), 36–45.

Shalley, CE 1995. 'Effects of coaction, expected evaluation, and goal setting on creativity and productivity', *Academy of Management Journal*, 38(2), 483–503.

Thamhain, HJ 2003. 'Managing innovative R&D teams', *R&D Management*, 33(3), 297–311.

# Part IV

Hunter, ST, Bedell, KE & Mumford, MD 2007. 'Climate for creativity: A quantitative review', *Creativity Research Journal*, 19(1), 69–90.

## Chapter 11: Risk-taking

'50 most powerful women in business: 5. Sue Lloyd-Hurwitz', *The Australian*, 20 February 2015. Retrieved from http://www.theaustralian.com.au/business/the-deal-magazine/most-powerful-women-in-business-5-susan-lloyd-hurwitz/story-e6frgabx-1227221176817.

Allspaw, J 2012. 'Blameless postmortems and a just culture', Etsy, 22 May. Retrieved from https://codeascraft.com/2012/05/22/blameless-postmortems/.

Carroll, R 2014. 'Silicon Valley's culture of failure ... and "the walking dead" it leaves behind', *The Guardian Australia*, 29 June. Retrieved from http://www.theguardian.com/technology/2014/jun/28/silicon-valley-startup-failure-culture-success-myth.

Chacko, P 2011. 'Innovista time again', TATA. Retrieved from http://www.tata.com/lead/innovista_time.htm.

Chacko, P 2011. 'Jelly for the belly', TATA, August. Retrieved from http://www.tata.com/company/articlesinside/!$$$!nvD08yOd78=/TLYVr3YPkMU=.

Dewett, T 2006. 'Exploring the role of risk in employee creativity', *Journal of Creative Behavior*, 40(1), 27–45.

Engineers Without Borders, http://www.ewb.ca/.

Engineers Without Borders 2008. 'Admitting failure'. Retrieved from http://www.ewb.ca/ideas/admitting-failure-0.

Higgins, ET 1998. 'Promotion and prevention: Regulatory focus as a motivational principle', in MP Zanna (ed.) *Advances in Experimental Social Psychology*, Academic Press, USA.

Janssen, O & Van Yperen, NW 2004. 'Employees' goal orientations, the quality of leader-member exchange, and the outcomes of job performance and job satisfaction', *Academy of Management Journal*, 47, 368–384.

Morris, L 2009. 'Celebrating failure (intelligent failure that is)', Innovation Labs, 3 December. Retrieved from http://www.innovationlabs.com/2009/12/tata-innovista/.

Mueller, JS, Melwani, S & Goncalo, JA 2011. 'The bias against creativity: why people desire but reject creative ideas', *Psychological Science*. Retrieved from http://digitalcommons.ilr.cornell.edu/cgi/viewcontent.cgi?article=1457&context=articles.

Ouschan, L, Boldero, JM, Kashima, Y, Wakimoto, R et al. S 2007. 'Regulatory focus strategies scale: A measure of individual differences in the endorsement of regulatory strategies', *Asian Journal of Social Psychology*, 10(4), 243–257.

Thomas, O 2012. 'Etsy's winning secret: Don't play the blame game!' *Business Insider Australia*, 16 May. Retrieved from http://www.businessinsider.com.au/etsy-chad-dickerson-blameless-post-mortem-2012-5.

Wilson, J 2013. 'Viagra: The little blue pill that could', CNN, 27 March. Retrieved from http://edition.cnn.com/2013/03/27/health/viagra-anniversary-timeline/index.html.

## Chapter 12: Cohesion

Bass, BM & Avolio, BJ 1994. *Improving organizational effectiveness through transformational leadership*, Sage, USA.

da Costa, S, Páez, D, Sánchez, F, Gondim, S et al. 2014. 'Factors favoring innovation in organizations: An integration of meta-analyses', *Revista de Psicología del Trabajo y de las Organizaciones*, 30(2), 67–74.

Hunter, ST, Bedell, KE & Mumford, MD 2007. 'Climate for creativity: A quantitative review', *Creativity Research Journal*, 19(1), 69–90.

Smith, B 2014. 'Innovating at scale: Creating common purpose', Intuit, 15 January. Retrieved from http://network.intuit. com/2014/01/15/innovating-at-scale/.

### Chapter 13: Participation

Arrington, M 2008. 'Yahoo to close Brickhouse by end of year', *Tech Crunch*, 9 December. Retrieved from http://techcrunch. com/2008/12/09/yahoo-to-close-brickhouse-by-end-of-year/.

Baumeister, Roy 2002. 'Ego depletion and self-control failure: An energy model of the self's executive function', *Self and Identity* 1(2), 129–136.

Bock, L 2015. *Work Rules! Insights from inside Google that will transform how you live and lead*, Hodder and Stoughton, UK.

Castiaux, A & Paque, S 2009. 'Participative innovation: When innovation becomes everyone's business', *International Journal of Entrepreneurship and Innovation Management*, 10(2), 111–121.

Ries, E 2011. *The lean startup: How today's entrepreneurs use continuous innovation to create radically successful businesses*, Random House LLC, USA.

Sheeran, P 2002. 'Intention-behavior relations: A conceptual and empirical review', *European Review of Social Psychology*, 12(1), 1–36.

Vlaskovits, P 2011. 'Henry Ford, innovation, and that "faster horse" quote', *Harvard Business Review*, 29 August. Retrieved from https://hbr.org/2011/08/henry-ford-never-said-the-fast/.

## Further reading

Agrell, A & Gustafson, R 1994. 'The Team Climate Inventory (TCI) and group innovation: A psychometric test on a Swedish sample of work groups', *Journal of Occupational & Organizational Psychology*, 67(2), 143–151.

Anderson, NR & West, MA 1998. 'Measuring climate for work group innovation: Development and validation of the team climate inventory', *Journal of Organizational Behavior*, 19(3), 235–258.

Axtell, CM, Holman, DJ, Unsworth, KL, Wall, TD et al. 2000. 'Shopfloor innovation: Facilitating the suggestion and implementation of ideas', *Journal of Occupational & Organizational Psychology*, 73(3), 265–385.

Bain, PG, Mann, L & Pirola-Merlo, A 2001. 'The innovation imperative: The relationships between team climate, innovation, and performance in research and development teams', *Small Group Research*, 32(1), 55–73.

Burningham, C & West, MA 1995. 'Individual, climate, and group interaction processes as predictors of work team innovation', *Small Group Research*, 26(1), 106–117.

Farr, JL & West, MA 1990. *Innovation and creativity at work: Psychological and organizational strategies*, John Wiley & Sons, USA.

Plunkett, D 1990. 'The creative organization: An empirical investigation of the importance of participation in decision-making', *Journal of Creative Behavior*, 24(2), 140–148.

## Chapter 14: Physical environment

Atchley, RA, Strayer, DL, Atchley, P 2012. 'Creativity in the wild: Improving creative reasoning through immersion in natural settings', *PLoS ONE*, 7(12).

BHP Billiton, 2012. 'Resourcing the future', via *Australian Financial Review*, 8 July 2012. Retrieved from http://www.afr.com/rw/2009-2014/AFR/2012/07/08/Photos/09a66320-c8cb-11e1-a18b-e5c71f70dca5_BHP_City_Square.pdf.

Clapham, MM 2001. 'The effects of affect manipulation and information exposure on divergent thinking', *Creativity Research Journal*, 13, 335–350.

Knight, CS & Haslam, A 2010. 'The relative merits of lean, enriched, and empowered offices: An experimental examination of the impact of workspace management strategies on well-being and productivity', *Journal of Experimental Psychology: Applied*, 16(2), 158.

Lichtenfeld, S, Elliot, A, Maier, M & Pekrun, R 2012. 'Fertile green: Green facilitates creative performance', *Personality and Social Psychology Bulletin*, 38 (6), 784–797.

McCoy, JM & Evans, GW 2002. 'The potential role of the physical environment in fostering creativity', *Creativity Research Journal*, 14(3–4), 409–426.

Mehta, R, Zhu, R & Cheema, A 2012. 'Is noise always bad? Exploring the effects of ambient noise on creative cognition', *Journal of Consumer Research*, 39, 784–99.

Nieuwenhuis, M, Knight, C, Postmes, T & Haslam, SA 2014. 'The relative benefits of green versus lean office space: Three field experiments', *Journal of Experimental Psychology: Applied*, 20(3), 199–214.

Thayer, JF, Verkuil, B, Brosschot, JF, Kampschroer, K, et al. 2010. 'Effects of the physical work environment on physiological measures of stress', *European Journal of Cardiovascular Prevention & Rehabilitation*, 17 (4), 431–439.

Ulrich, RS, Simons, RF, Losito, BD, Fiorito, E et al. 1991. 'Stress recovery during exposure to natural and urban environments', *Journal of Environmental Psychology*, 11, 201–230.

University of British Columbia 2009. 'Effect of colors: Blue boosts creativity, while red enhances attention to detail', *ScienceDaily*, 6 February. Retrieved from www.sciencedaily.com/releases/2009/02/090205142143.htm.

## Further reading

Amabile, TM & Gitomer, J 1984. 'Children's artistic creativity effects of choice in task materials', *Personality and Social Psychology Bulletin*, 10(2), 209–215.

Amabile, TM & Gryszkiewicz, ND 1989. 'The creative environment scales: Work environment inventory', *Creativity Research Journal*, 2(4), 231–253.

Ceylan, C, Dul, J & Aytac, S 2008. 'Can the office environment stimulate a manager's creativity?', *Human Factors and Ergonomics in Manufacturing & Service Industries*, 18(6), 589–602.

Dubos, R 1971. 'Man made environments', *Journal of School Health*, 41(7), 339–343.

Dul, J & Ceylan, C 2014. 'The impact of a creativity-supporting work environment on a firm's product innovation performance', *Journal of Product Innovation Management*, 31(6), 1254–1267.

González, MSR, Fernández, CA & Cameselle, JMS 1997. 'Empirical validation of a model of user satisfaction with buildings and their environments as workplaces', *Journal of Environmental Psychology*, 17(1), 69–74.

Kaplan, R & Kaplan, S 1989. *The experience of nature: A psychological perspective*, CUP Archive.

Lewis, M & Moultrie, J 2005. 'The organizational innovation laboratory', *Creativity and Innovation Management*, 14(1), 73–83.

McCoy, JM & Evans, GW 2005. 'Physical work environment', in J Barling, EK Kelloway & MR Frone (eds) *Handbook of Work Stress*, Sage, USA.

Veitch, JA, Charles, KE, Farley, KM & Newsham, GR 2007. 'A model of satisfaction with open-plan office conditions: COPE field findings', *Journal of Environmental Psychology*, 27(3), 177–189.

Vischer, JC 2007. 'The effects of the physical environment on job performance: Towards a theoretical model of workspace stress', *Stress and Health*, 23(3), 175–184.

# INDEX

# *Connect with* WILEY ▶▶▶

WILEY

Browse and purchase the full range of Wiley publications on our official website.

**www.wiley.com**

Check out the Wiley blog for news, articles and information from Wiley and our authors.

**www.wileybizaus.com**

Join the conversation on Twitter and keep up to date on the latest news and events in business.

**@WileyBizAus**

Sign up for Wiley newsletters to learn about our latest publications, upcoming events and conferences, and discounts available to our customers.

**www.wiley.com/email**

Wiley titles are also produced in e-book formats. Available from all good retailers.

# Learn more with practical advice from our experts

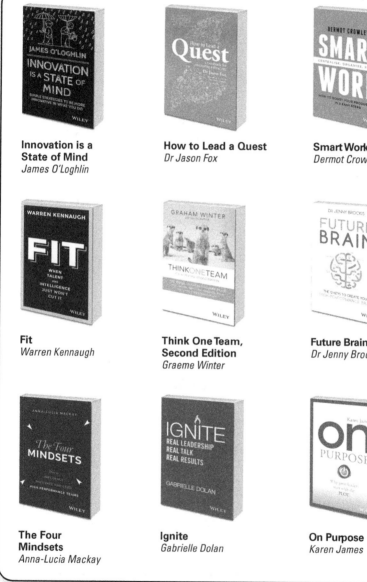

CPSIA information can be obtained
at www.ICGtesting.com
Printed in the USA
FSHW011219090620
71015FS

9 780730 326663